Hostage to History

The Cultural Collapse of the 21st Century Arab World

Elie Mikhael Nasrallah

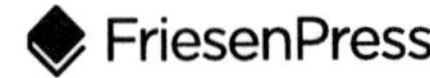

Suite 300 - 990 Fort St
Victoria, BC, Canada,V8V 3K2
www.friesenpress.com

First Edition — 2016

ISBN
978-1-4602-8277-9 (Hardcover)
978-1-4602-8278-6 (Paperback)
978-1-4602-8279-3 (eBook)

1. History, Middle East

Distributed to the trade by The Ingram Book Company

ACCLAIM FOR
Hostage to History

It's easy firing criticism from the outside—it takes enormous courage to do it from within. Elie Mikhael Nasrallah has guts. He also has something important to say.

—Roy MacGregor, author of *Canadians: Portrait of a County and Its People*

A complex socio-political study. . . intriguing, insightful, poignant, intellectually-driven, and mind-enriching. Elie M. Nasrallah says it all in the brilliant title of his latest book, *Hostage to History*.

How can a simplistic analysis be utilized in a region that—for many centuries—has been plagued by hegemonic regimes and ruthless forms of government? It is almost impossible to do! However, the author has genuinely endeavored to conduct a root cause analysis of the dilemmas and redundant debacles shadowing the Arab world while driving it into a deeper societal regression instead of seeking a renaissance that will sustain progress, promote growth, and ensure self-sufficiency.

Mr. Nasrallah's book covers many sensitive facets, some of which are untouchable in the Arab world. . . . Be it religious indoctrination and bigotry, sectarianism, illiteracy, sexual repression and gender discrimination, poverty and malnutrition, environmental mischiefs, economic injustice, and more! A comparative model is drawn between the ailing Arab world and other evolving yet stable societies. Subsequently, the book offers numerous corrective actions based on constructive self-critique, accountability, assuming responsibility, and fostering a collective willingness to overcome monumental hurdles while adopting a versatile socio-economic system with embedded democratic and humanistic values.

The author's extensive work is commendable, his output offers added value in understanding contemporary events, and his findings/recommendations are merited.

—Ghassan H. Elias, activist and Professor of Engineering, California State University, Northridge (CSUN), Los Angeles

The Arab world is in turmoil, real turmoil. Since the "Arab Spring" started, ignited by the self-immolation of Tunisian fruit seller Mohamed Bouazizi in December 2010, dictators have been toppled and totalitarian regimes have crumbled. Democracy, however, which many around the world hoped would replace those regimes, never came. Instead, extremist Islamism sprouted, accompanied by mass killings, ethnic and religious cleansing, and suppression of freedoms. What went wrong?

In *Hostage to History,* Elie Mikhael Nasrallah seeks to understand and explain the reasons for the failure of the Arab states. He virtually "scans" the Arab body politic to identify the causes of this tragic situation and find a realistic remedy. Born and raised in Lebanon and having lived in Canada for decades, therefore knowing the Arab culture in depth and having been immersed in the Western way of reasoning and thinking, the author is capable of assessing the status of the Arab world as an "insider from the outside"!

This book offers an objective explanation of the causes that led to this state of affairs in the Arab World, focusing on the role Arab culture played as a catalyst. Mr. Nasrallah offers a roadmap that can help restore order and progressively establish a democratic system based on the culture and traditions of the region. An excellent in-depth analysis and a praiseworthy initiative!

—Massoud Maalouf, former Ambassador of
Lebanon to Canada, Poland, and Chile

Provocative yet inviting discussion, Nasrallah has taken a bold step to ignite accountability in the Arab world. Inspired by his origin, he paints a bleak picture of the failings caused by a sick culture that rewards few and represses many. Those who are in positions of authority in the Middle East need to look in the mirror, join the discussion, and be the agents of change that Nasrallah pleads will lead the Reformation. He even provides a twelve-point prescription for the sick patient.

—Warren L. Creates, B.A., LL.B.

This book is dedicated to my wife Nancy

A capacity, and taste, for reading, gives access to whatever has already been discovered by others. It is the key, or one of the keys, to the already solved problems. And not only so, it gives a relish, and facility, for successful pursuing the [yet] unsolved ones.

—Abraham Lincoln (September 30, 1859)

If the only options we want to support and assist are either the old-style dictatorships or an angry scattering of closed ethnic enclaves, then we are denying the Middle East's citizens exactly the sort of pluralism that has allowed our societies to thrive.

—Doug Saunders, *The Globe and Mail*

In the 1,000 years since the reign of Caliph Mamoun, say the authors, the Arabs have translated as many books as Spain translates in one year.

—*The Economist,* referring to the 2002 UN Arab Human Development Report

Table of Contents

Introduction

Dr. Paul Kalanithi, a neurosurgeon who died at the age of 37, wrote these mesmerizing sentences after seeing his own CT scan:

> As soon as the CT scan was done, I began reviewing the images. The diagnosis was immediate: Masses matting the lungs and deforming the spine. Cancer. In my neurosurgical training, I had reviewed hundreds of scans for fellow doctors to see if surgery offered any hope. I'd scribble in the chart "Widely metastatic disease—no role for surgery," and move on. But this scan was different: It was my own.[1]

In similar fashion, like a social science surgeon, Egyptian writer Mohammed H. Heikal examined the UN's 2003 Arab Human Development Report—a "CT scan" of the Arab world—with alarming tone and urgency. This was his diagnosis:

> The bell rung by the AHDR and heard by Arabs and other people the world over carried echoes of all the bells ringing through our lives. It was a call to knowledge and learning, an announcement of the last chance to join the trip to the future, an appeal for cleansing, an injunction to make way for an urgent priority, and finally a forewarning of imminent danger—urging us to

> hasten to douse the flames of a still-small fire waiting to engulf the region in a formidable blaze.
>
> —Mohammad Hassanein Heikal — Egyptian writer — (2003), on The Arab Human Develpoment Report by the U.N.

This book is an updated virtual CT scan for the ailing Arab body politic. It shows the growth of a cancer that is spreading into many parts. My analysis has led me to conclude that surgery is both necessary and urgent. Time is running out. The scribble on the chart should read, "To the operating room—now!"

On June 2, 2015, while sitting at a café in Ottawa, Canada's capital, I decided to check the news from the Middle East by reading the *Washington Post* online. The *Post* reported the following story: "Videos posted on social media accounts allied with the Islamic State showed the group in control of checkpoints in the small town of Sawran. One image showed four decapitated heads tossed into the back of a truck." Similar headlines had dominated newspapers over the past year, and they have been dominating them ever since. There's no question: The assassins are hard at work. The merchants of death are advancing. The barbaric squad is sowing fear and tyranny. The savagery of blind belief is spreading its venom. Minorities are being slaughtered like sheep. Sectarian strife is raging like a brushfire, and the Arab world is collapsing, sucked into a black hole of cosmic dimensions. The end of that civilization is all but assured.

"Daesh has a mother: the invasion of Iraq," wrote Kamel Daoud in The New York Times on November 20, 2015. "But it also has a father: Saudi Arabia and its religious-industrial complex." Moreover, I may add, the air, the water, the food and the infrastructure of its daily living were all provided for by a historical narrative of a culture which is in deep crisis since the end of its Golden Age and its continuing war

with modernity. *(Title: "Saudi Arabia, An ISIS That Has Made It.")*

One of the most intriguing questions in contemporary international affairs is, *why?* Why has the Arab world descended into its current state of political upheaval, total meltdown, and economic stagnation when, historically, it has produced so many scientific and literary accomplishments? This leads to another recurring question: Is it possible to envision the establishment of a liberal democracy in a land that has no experience with such principles, no separation of religion and politics, no freedom, no women's rights, no modern educational system, and where illiteracy is more than twenty-five percent and unemployment is in the thirty percent range? How about a land where seventy percent of the population is under thirty years of age and one-third of the population is below fifteen years of age? That was the dream of the Arab Spring in 2011, but since then, reality has taken over.

On December 17, 2010, Mohamed Bouazizi, a Tunisian fruit vendor, set himself on fire to protest the confiscation of his belongings, protesting the injustices of the status quo and the humiliation visited upon him by local authorities, which represented an authoritarian regime. His public self-immolation became the catalyst for the Tunisian revolution and the beginning of the so-called Arab Spring. Since then, the Arab world has resembled a burning bush of historic and catastrophic proportions. Throughout that period, the rest of the world has been asking, *why?*

What is wrong, really wrong, with the Arab world? Why is the Arab Middle East one of the sickest regions of the globe? What is behind its constant upheaval, export of terrorism, ethnic cleansing, barbaric execution of minorities, religious strife, animosity against modernity, subjugation of women, suppression of freedom, lack of scientific progress and innovative thinking, dependency on importing all major technological and advanced know-how from the West while also, in turn, hating it? Where is the life in this ancient part of the human race? What went wrong with Arab civilization?

Terrorist groups like ISIS are threatening not only the international political and economic system but also the fabric of citizens' everyday lives. They attacked an art exhibit in Texas in May 2015. They threatened to attack shopping centres in North America, Europe, and Asia and are threatening to converge on Rome to attack it, because, to them at least, it represents Christian civilization. In fact, the November 13th, 2015 terrorists attacks in Paris, France, and Beirut, were the most barbaric examples of how that cult of death has taken roots in some quarters in modern times. Wave upon wave of refugees from Syria, the wider Middle East and Africa, hundreds of thousands of them, are flooding European shores, and the photos of toddlers drowning and being washed onto beaches and children and women crying and crossing the oceans for a better life is only the beginning.

The disintegration of the Arab state system, which was created after the breakdown of the Ottoman empire in 1918, the savage strife between the Shia and Sunni sects of Islam in Syria, Iraq, Yemen, Libya, and beyond, and the total reversal of the promise of the Arab Spring into an endless nightmare all invite the question: What on Earth is behind this historic meltdown and catastrophic collapse of Arab nation-states in contrast to progressive trends in most other areas of the world?

The thesis of this timely book is simple: *It's the culture, stupid!* (To borrow from Bill Clinton's famous 1992 Presidential campaign slogan, "It's the economy, stupid!") This book posits the view that Arab culture is the driving force behind this destabilizing, destructive, and deadly period in the history of the Arab region as it relates to the global challenges of modernity and advancement.

What is culture?

> Culture: The system of shared beliefs, values, customs, behaviours, and artifacts that the members of society use to cope with their world and with one another, and that are transmitted from generation to generation through learning.[2]

> Culture refers to those shared beliefs that people learn from society. While all human beings hold beliefs, they do not all hold the same beliefs. Members of the same culture acquire a common belief system. Those shared beliefs also set norms—expectations of how people are expected to behave. . . . Cultural identity has two sets of sources. The Greeks distinguished these two sources by the terms ethnos and ethos. Ethnos refers to the biological ties of ethnicity that binds people together. When applied to nationality it also includes a common language and heritage. Ethos refers to the intellectual ties that hold people together—of religion, ideology, or patriotism.
>
> (Source: www.civicvoices.org.)

The objective of this book is to show that what is really going on in the Arab world is not as advertised by popular media, politicians, local warlords, tyrants, or stale editorials. It is imperative to understand the causes and hidden currents behind events so we can isolate them in the quest for workable solutions.

From this perspective, this book is a call for realism as well as an affirmation of the thesis that cultural forces in the Arab world are rooted deep in its history and obdurate to changing modern currents. Thus, the outcome of any military action that seeks to force change from outside is as difficult to predict as the weather in Canada in 2077! Make no mistake:

Following his Syrian military adventure, Russian President Vladimir Putin will, in due course, like the precedent set by United States and Europe, find out the authenticity of this axiom and come to regret his intervention, as many other empires have discovered in the Arab Middle East.

George F. Kennan, in his historic and time-tested 1947 essay, "The Sources of Soviet Conduct," which predicted the gradual decay and eventual collapse of the Soviet Union over forty years before it happened, advanced the thesis that "The possibility remains (and in the opinion of this writer it is a strong one) that Soviet power, like the capitalist world of its conception, bears within it the seeds of its own decay, and that the sprouting of these seeds is well advanced."[3]

Likewise, the cultural decay of the Arab world is now upon us and is becoming a menace to world order. Unlike the Soviet Union, however, the cultural crash in Arab lands is not an ideology to be contained, a military power to be checked, or an economic powerhouse to be tamed. No containment policy is needed or desired, because the indigenous forces it contains are hostile to outside manipulation and control. Janice G. Stein, professor of political science at the University of Toronto and a founding director of the Munk School of Global Affairs, offered this pertinent analysis regarding the challenges facing the international community in trying to fix the disorder of failed Arab states:

> The crux of the problem isn't simply trying to put back together failed and failing states. It is much more challenging. What is important isn't just that Syria is riddled with violent conflict, as are large parts of Iraq; it's that the order that governed this part of the world for the past 100 years is breaking apart. The capacity to re-engineer these broken societies has to come from inside the regions. The old order, where

governance solutions can be imposed from outside, is gone for good.[4]

Little can be done when we survey the minefields in the Arab political, social, and religious landscape and find that:

- The Sunni/Shia religious war is being fought on the basis of seventh century ideas, culture, and civilization. Tribalism, sectarianism, and family kinship are paramount. In fact, Islam's battle with modernity seems to be raging on all fronts.
- Totalitarian regimes and authoritarian and monarchist governments have sucked the oxygen out of civil society and left it an empty shell. In fact, they created after decades in power what could be called "political and cultural deserts." This is why we see the regimes who are hanging on to power saying, "Either us or the flood: ISIS and Hell!"
- Arab countries are inebriated by oil and lack a transition plan from this destructive dependency on this single resource to a more modern, productive economic system that enables them to compete in the world of ideas, innovation, and progress.
- The concept of citizenship is as fleeting as a fish in a lake, and civic life, the public square, the media, and the educational system are in the hands of a tyrant or a gang of autocratic family members resembling a mafia dynasty.
- The rule of law is as absent as snow in the desert, with corruption running deep into the culture of most Arab political, bureaucratic, and economic institutions. Iraq, Syria, and Lebanon are prime examples, especially Iraq before and after the American invasion. Little can be done from outside when concepts like diversity, tolerance, and acceptance of the other are interpreted as weakness and thought of as alien cultural invasion.

- The game of blaming foreigners for all that ails the culture and society is a 24/7 sport. In fact, it is similar to a long Western movie, repeated again and again. Human nature's most destructive vices are all present at once: resentment, orthodoxy, and scapegoating.
- The truth is still considered the exclusive domain of authority, be it religious, political or social. Unilateralism in religious faith is transformed to the political arena. The regime, the leader, is god on Earth.
- Millions of young people are restless, leaderless, and jobless. Consider that sixty percent of the Arab world is under the age of thirty. They represent a ticking demographic time bomb, especially in Egypt, where the median age is twenty-five, as well as in Syria, Saudi Arabia, and Yemen.
- Women, who comprise half the population, are invisible in the public square, in the political arena, and in places of power and many of them are illiterate.
- The majority regards reading, translation of foreign books, and acceptance of new and challenging ideas, concepts, and modern ways as unacceptable foreign influences invading the Arab body politic.
- The society worships tradition, history, Salafi, [strict adherence to theological principles and sharia law, and is against innovation in interpretation of religious doctrines] and the old, tired ways by making them sacred and unalterable. Little can be done when most people still believe in superstition, myth worship, and ancient unscientific methods. Fortune telling is a huge business in Lebanon, Egypt, Syria, Morocco, and other states.

From this perspective, Zbigniew Brzezinski, national security advisor in the Carter administration, was prescient when he wrote that: "The transformation of the Middle East will be a more complex undertaking than the restoration of postwar Europe. After all, social restoration is inherently easier than transformation. Islamic traditions, religious convictions and cultural habits must be treated with patient respect. Only then will the time be ripe for democracy in the Middle East."[5]

Any such transformation, however, must start, first and foremost, from inside the Arab world. Transporting or imposing democracy as if it is a trophy to be bought is not only impractical, it is also dangerous. For instance, the phenomenon of the Islamic State of Iraq and Syria (ISIS), which is trying to create a "caliphate" in Iraq and Syria, is no accident. It is a symptom of a deep-seated decay in the infrastructure of the Arab body politic. "What is most striking, though, is how much Al-Meshar sees ISIS not as just a religious problem but as the product of all the problems ailing this region: underdevelopment, sectarianism, lagging education, sexual repression, lack of respect for women and lack of pluralism in all intellectual thought."[6]

Therefore, in the absence of what the world commonly regards as rationalism and its application in the Arab political culture, it is no wonder that the Arab Spring was like a seed that fell on stony ground. The great philosopher Baruch Spinoza was correct when he wrote 360 years ago about reason, democracy, and government, as Rebecca Newberger Goldstein points out in a piece for the *New York Times:*

> It is for this reason that he [Spinoza] argued that a government that impedes the development of the sciences subverts the very grounds for state legitimacy, which is to provide us physical safety so that we can realize our full potential. And this, too, is why he argued so adamantly against the influence of clerics in government. Statecraft infused with religion not only dissolves the justification for the state

> but is intrinsically unstable, since it must insist on its version of the truth against all others.[7]

In his ground-breaking book *Orientalism,* Edward W. Said defined the term as the acceptance in the West of "the basic distinction between East and West as the starting point for elaborate theories, epics, novels, social descriptions, and political accounts concerning the Orient, its people, customs, 'mind,' destiny and so on."[8] That Orientalism was condescending and offered a distorted worldview of the Arab Middle East is beyond question. Orientalism is a way of seeing that imagines, emphasizes, exaggerates, and distorts the differences of Arab peoples and cultures as compared to that of Europe and the US. It often involves seeing Arab culture as exotic, backward, uncivilized, and, at times, dangerous. In my case, I am writing about the Arab world not as an outsider with an agenda, a complex of some sort, or a hidden political or social motivation but as a son, as a citizen, as a man who was born in Lebanon, which is considered to be a microcosm of the region. I write out of utter perplexity, concern, and bewilderment regarding the state of the Arab world, which has descended into a dark age.

Human nature being the same everywhere, there is no such thing as a superior race, group, or ethnic origin. What separates one person from another is the cultural context, history of development, and geographic imperatives. It has been said that to live is to sink roots. "Not only do you occupy a certain place, but that place, in turn, occupies you. Its culture shapes the way you see the world, its language informs the way you think, its customs structure you as a social being. Who you ultimately are is determined to an important degree by the vast web of entanglements of 'home'"[9]

By delving deep into the cultural background of the Arab world, this book seeks to understand and, hopefully, find a way out of this difficult period of history. The Arab peoples, the younger generations, and people all over the world want and need to know the answers to these daunting questions.

In the coming chapters, I will explore the origins of the Arab cultural collapse by revisiting the fateful clash between the rationalist and anti-rationalist schools of thought in the thirteenth century, when the Golden Age of the Arab Empire came to an end. Many will be surprised to learn that between the eighth and tenth centuries, reason and science flourished in cities like Basra and Baghdad under the Mu'tazila school of thought, leading to several significant scientific discoveries. After the tenth century, this rationalist movement declined, and the anti-rationalist camp—the Ash'ari—became the dominant religious and cultural force, and it has remained in this position ever since. I will also discuss the modern problems that the Arab culture and peoples confront, especially regarding illiteracy, women's suppression, sexuality, religion, oil, economic stagnation, lack of interest in science, demographic challenges, and a variety of other relevant issues.

In conclusion, it must be stressed that this analysis and critique, this "CT scan" of the failing of the cultural contents of the Arab world, in light of the crash of the Arab Spring, are not dirty laundry that is exhibited for pleasure or satisfaction. Rather, this book attempts what Socrates once described as the job of a philosopher from the inside pretending to be an outsider in order to show, tell, and explore the truth of his community.

> Socrates turned himself into an outsider in his own city, but didn't move to another. . . . There is in every community something that has to remain unsaid, unnamed, unuttered, and you signal your belonging to that community precisely by participating in the general silence. Revealing everything, 'telling all,' is a foreigner's job. Either because foreigners do not know the local cultural codes or because they are not

> bound to respect them, they can afford to be outspoken.[10]

That being said, the philosopher becomes a metaphysical gypsy. I am, thus, the insider turned outsider to tell a story about a culture that was once great but is now crashing, collapsing in a cataclysmic cosmic fashion. I do this in the hope that properly diagnosing the illness that afflicts this culture can lead us to a prescription that will enable it to return to greatness once again. Indeed, the inspirational quote below is a great start to that journey.

> "Go for broke. Always try and do too much. Dispense with safety nets. Take a deep breath before you begin talking. Aim for the stars. Keep grinning. Be bloody-minded. Argue with the world. And never forget that writing is as close as we get to keeping a hold on the thousand and one things—childhood, certainties, cities, doubts, dreams, instants, phrases, parents, loves—that go on slipping, like sand, through our fingers."
>
> —Salman Rushdie

To readers: This book is about Arab culture and not about Islam or Islamic theology. The inter-changing usage of Islam/Arab, Muslim/Arab, or Islamic/Arab culture is meant to emphasize the point that Islam is adhered to by 95 per cent of the Arab world which is of 400 million Arabs. Like scholars and authors, Reza Aslan and Fareed Zakaria, both Muslims, I am of the opinion that culture and not faith is the driving force behind historical and recent events in the Arab Middle East. It is my belief also, that people use their cultural lenses to read their religious texts and view the world at large. Hence the periodic conflation and reference to Arab culture and Islamic faith.

Chapter 1.

The Arab World 101: Culture Crash Course

The present was an egg laid by the past that had the future inside its shell.

—Zora Hurston

The only people who see the whole picture are the ones who step outside the frame.

—Salman Rushdie

Henry Kissinger observed that in the political realm, two basic elements must be mastered in order to manage events: first, demographic trends; second, human psychology and the management of people. This observation could not be more pertinent to our examination and analysis of the sick state of the Arab world. Fateful demographic developments and divisive human relations between the governed masses and the governing elites, between various sectarian segments, and between different generations are on display daily.

The Arab Middle East is the sick state system in the modern world. The daily dose of incessant upheaval and atrocities, sectarian divisions, barbaric slaughtering of minorities, medieval treatment of women, and the utter madness of the whole disintegrating body politic of the Arab world is unbearable to concerned citizens around the globe and to those born in the region or who are interested in its affairs.

Moreover, let us define and have a context for our examination of the Arab world. What constitutes, defines, and makes up this entity? In plain language, what do we mean by the term "Arab world"?

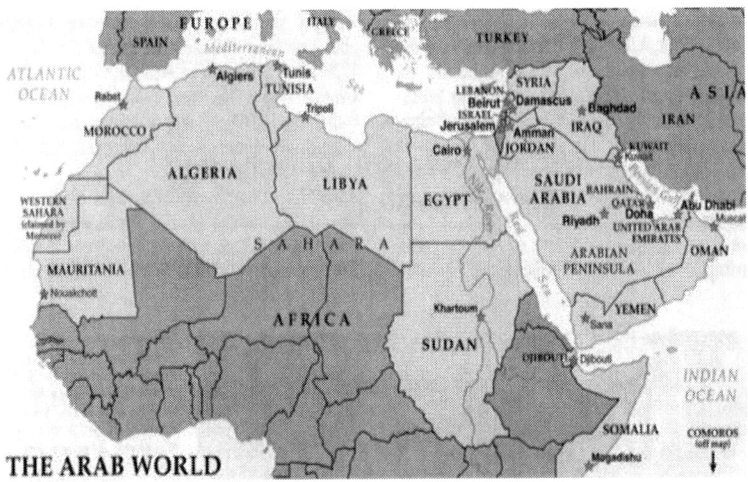

THE ARAB WORLD

- The Arab world stretches from Morocco across Northern Africa to the Persian Gulf. The Arab world is more or less equal to the area known as the Middle East and North Africa (MENA), although this excludes Somalia, Djibouti, and the Comoros Islands, which are also part of the Arab world.
- There are twenty-two Arab countries/areas: Algeria, Bahrain, the Comoros Islands, Djibouti, Egypt, Iraq, Jordan, Kuwait, Lebanon, Libya, Morocco, Mauritania, Oman, Palestine, Qatar, Saudi Arabia, Somalia, Sudan, Syria, Tunisia, United Arab Emirates, and Yemen. Contrary to popular belief, Iran and Turkey *are not* Arab countries;.[11]Iran is Persian, Turkey is Turkish.

Arab,Turkish and Persian civilizations came and gone, co-operated and fought with one another for centuries.

- The Arab world can also be defined as those countries where Arabic is the dominant language.
- Arab countries are religiously and ethnically diverse, although Islam is the dominant religion in most Arab countries.

Now that we know where the Arab world is located, the following shall serve as a background to many basic fundamental social and moral value systems for most of the Arab world.

Understanding Arab Culture

Two fundamental facets of this subject must be stated at the outset: First, Arab culture and the Islamic faith are deeply intertwined. Second, Islam is the single most dominant influence in the Arab world. Therefore, discerning Arab culture from Islamic culture is a tricky business. But the fact remains, that Arab culture is different from, shall we say Indonesia, India and other major Islamic cultures and states. The Arabic language, history, geography, traditions, memories, and other variables all conspire to create a cultural nerrative that is specific to Arabic-speaking countries. Moreover, although Arab culture is homogenous with regional differences, ethnic groups and religions, there are general overarching characteristics that are Arabic-specific and culturally-oriented.

Arabic Beliefs

Ingrained in the Arab consciousness is the idea that God controls most things in life. Every person should believe in God and have a religious affiliation. There is no place for atheists or agnostics. Humans cannot control most events, and fate determines one's life. There should be no separation between church/mosque and state. Religion should be taught in schools and promoted by government. Moreover, Arabs share basic beliefs and values that cross national and social boundaries. Personal beliefs are influenced by Islam and are shared by non-Muslims. Piety is one of the most admirable characteristics in a person. Religious tenets should not be subjected to liberal interpretations. Islamic law (sharia) takes precedent over all other law. There should be no threat to established beliefs.

Arabic Values

In the Arab world, a person's dignity, honor, and reputation are of paramount importance. It is vital as well to behave at all times in a way that creates a good impression. Loyalty to one's family takes precedence over personal needs, loyalty to friends, or the demands of a job. A strong family structure is vital, as are clearly defined roles for male and female children. Children are considered the "jewels" of the family. It is held that wisdom increases with age, and inherent roles and responsibilities of men and women are vastly different. Furthermore, social class and family background are the major determining factors of personal status, followed by individual character and achievement.

Arabic Self-perceptions

Arabs have a rich history of literature, medicine, art, mathematics, and science. They are generous, humanitarian, polite, and loyal. They constitute what is known as the "Arab nation." They also mistrust many Western values and see them as having a corrupting influence on their culture. Many also feel that the West is exploiting Arabs.

Arabic Traditions

Western culture emphasizes the notion that actions speak louder than words. In the Arab culture, it is believed that words without action have value, as they can play a role in avoiding conflict and saving face. Never expect a "yes" or "no" answer to a sensitive matter. The answer may be somewhere in between. It is discourteous to say "no," and sometimes "yes" may mean "maybe." The phrase "As God wills it" may mean "no" in many instances. And the sentence "Do this for my sake" will incur indebtedness.

Arabs tend to provide details about their lives and connections. Honor and dignity flow from the family. A high value is placed on friendship, and if a friend is in need, one must help as much as possible. Moreover, Arabs are socially oriented and like to be praised in public. People who establish relationships are the most successful. One must sound sincere. Above all, pride is one of the mainstays of the Arab character.

Arabic Thinking

Subjectivity and emotional outbursts are common in Arab culture and deemed acceptable. Subjective perceptions are allowed to direct actions and are considered acceptable. Admitting an error is rare if it will cause a loss of face socially. Honor is more important than facts. Arabs value and believe in individuals more than institutions. Patience is critical and valued; Arabs have plenty of time. There is little need to accommodate people in a hurry.[12]

The Arab Culture in Modern Times

Is culture destiny? Is there something exceptionally alarming and undoubtedly evident in the Arab world that has set it on a collision course with modernity? Are we to conclude that nothing short of a dramatic shift and a total reformation of the Arab political culture is needed to escape the gravitational pull of this black hole? The answer is yes, yes, and yes!

> To live is to sink roots. Life is possible only to the extent that you find a place hospitable enough to receive you and allow you to settle down. What follows is a sort of symbiosis: Just as you grow into the world, the world grows into you. Not only do you occupy a certain place, but that place, in turn, occupies you. Its culture shapes the way you see the world, its language informs the way you think, its customs structure you as a social being. Who you ultimately are is determined to an important degree by the vast web of entanglements of "home."[13]

The culture of that "home" to about 400 million inhabitants of the Arab world could be a blessing or a curse. Certainly, it was a blessing at the height of Arab Empire of power and influence in the Middle Ages. The Islamic Golden Age flourished when various caliphates experienced unprecedented scientific, economic, and cultural advancement, only to end with the destruction of the Abbasid dynasty at the hands of the Mongol invaders and the destruction of Baghdad in 1258. However, some scholars contend that the Islamic Golden Age extended even to the fifteenth century. Then Western civilization took over and has continued to dominate the world until the present day. The following passage provides a great context to the thesis at issue:

> The highest tide of Islamic culture, 800 to 1100 A.D., was coincident with the lowest ebb of European culture. While the Muslims enjoyed general standards of living equal to if not surpassing those of the preceding Graeco-Roman civilization, the Europeans were living in the semi-barbarous squalor and restricted regime of feudalism—a pattern unalleviated by comforts and luxuries.
>
> These centuries of European history have aptly been termed the Dark Ages. The Church alone kept alive sparks of learning amidst the ashes left by the barbaric hordes of Goths. It took centuries for Latin Europe to digest this illiterate mass of barbarism and to assimilate it into a vital and intelligent organism capable of progress.
>
> One of the strangest dramas of history is that at the very moment when Europe, prodded by contacts with the Islamic culture in Sicily and Spain and by the Crusades, began to recover from its prolonged descent toward darkness, Islam entered a decline that was to carry it down into the very fog of obscurantism from which it had helped to rescue Europe.[14]

The culture that produced a golden global civilization in the past is now a curse and a cause for concern. How did we get here? How did the same cultural characteristics of one civilization produce such contradictory and conflicting outcomes?

> The point has often been made—if Islam is an obstacle to freedom, to science, to economic development, how it is that Muslim society

> in the past was a pioneer in all three, and this when Muslims were much closer in time to the sources and inspiration of their faith than they are now? Some have indeed posed the question is a different form—not "What has Islam done to the Muslims?" but "What have the Muslims done to Islam?" and have answered by laying the blame on specific teachers and doctrines and groups.[15]

The blame game has been the ultimate sport in Arab lands since the fall of the Arab empire. The Mongols, the Turks, the imperialists, the Jews, the Americans—it never ends, and it never answers any question or offers any solution to the countless predicaments and catastrophes visiting the Arab landscape nowadays. The dead hand of the past seems to influence every conversation, vision, and strategy for the future. This endless obsession with and rehearsal of the past is a disease that has been eating away at the Arab body politic since the end of the colonial era. "Poisoned by colonialism, stymied by Islam's battle with modernity, inebriated by oil, blocked by the absence of institutions that can mediate the fury of tribe and ethnicity, Middle Eastern states turn in circles. Syria is now the regional emblem, a vacuum in which only the violent nihilism of the jihadi thrives."[16]

The cultural heritage of the falling Arab-Islamic empire has certainly turned into a curse in modern times. Let us take a journey together into some of the most contested, controversial, and consequential questions and issues concerning Arab culture and modernity today.

1. Culture, defined in simple terms as a way of life, has imprisoned the minds of generations of Arab youth and adults who live in the glory of the distant past. History has been lived as a dream for so long that they cannot let it go. It replaces the agony of the present and negates the prospects of tomorrow.

2. Women are in exile within the "home" of culture. The predicament of women and their marginalization in the Arab world is a huge reason behind the decaying foundations of the Arab political, economic, and cultural palace.

In the early 1990s, Egyptian-American journalist Mona Eltahawy walked into the women's section on the metro in Cairo wearing a beige-and-red headscarf that framed her young face. A woman covered in a black veil that revealed only her eyes bristled with disapproval.

"Why aren't you wearing a niqab?" she asked.

"Isn't what I'm wearing enough?" Eltahawy asked. She had always found the niqab "terrifying" in its ability to render a woman invisible.

"If you want to eat a piece of candy," the woman said, "would you choose one that is in a wrapper or an unwrapped one?"

"I'm a woman, not a piece of candy," Eltahawy replied. (In *The Washinton Post* reviewing Eltahawy's book "Headscarves and Hymens on April 30, 2015, by Connie Schultz.)

It is not only the niqab that renders women invisible but also illiteracy, social norms, arranged marriages, patriarchy, religious dogma, and archaic mores, customs, and traditions.

Many women's rights and advances were rolled back after the Iranian revolution. "After Iran's 1979 Islamic revolution, women were barred from working as judges or attending soccer matches, forced to wear hijab, and declared unequal to men in the realms of inheritance, testimony and divorce—all under the pretext of hewing to Islamic tenets."[17] In fact, these and other backward-looking trends spread like wildfire around Arab societies and became what we see today, an awkward state for women's rights and place in the private and public spaces compared to other countries all over the globe. This is a fact that proves the interplay and interdependence of culture and religion in the Arab world. Iran, a Shia country, influenced the Arab world, mostly Sunni, after the said revolution in many ways. Till today, that equation is still in play daily.

3. Sex and sexuality are still taboos. Human nature was and is under siege in many parts of the Arab world. Honor killing is one manifestation of the problem of sexuality in the minds of the majority. Instead of celebrating, channelling, and coalescing the energy and utter pleasure of this undeniable human trait, generations of youth—men and women—are struggling to reconcile this basic human need with societal pressure and conformity. This is unhealthy physically, economically, and socially.

4. Critical inquiry and dissent are suppressed. In the Arab world, the tribe rules. It dominates the public sphere as well as the private domain. Conformity is suffocating talent, social change, and exposure to new ideas and practices, and it is making society stagnant and stale. New ideas are considered dangerous and undesirable. A contrarian is a pariah, holding his life in his hands. No freedom, no liberation of the self, only servitude and silence. In such a state, the individual is not productive, and society does not progress. In fact, it is regressing.

5. Servile deference to authority is demanded. Totalitarianism—the pursuit of total control over all aspects of public life—is a visible characteristic of the Arab landscape. Authority, be it religious, political, economic, or social, is revered and unduly respected as a social norm or a dictation of the culture. People must take the elders seriously, listen to them, adhere to their conclusions, and follow their advice even if it is evidently and manifestly wrong. If your father tells you that you

must not believe in evolution or that the moon landings are a myth, you must believe him. If the religious authority issues an order or dispenses advice, it is obligatory to follow the order and not question it.

6. Education emphasizes memorization and dictation, and it is state-controlled. Poor schools produce poor generations. Poor generations equal economic and social stagnation. Stagnation produces unemployed youth (sixty percent of the Arab world is under age twenty-five). Lazy youth means trouble, terrorism, and social decay.

7. The concept of citizenship is non-existent. It has been said widely that, excluding Egypt and Tunisia, all other Arab states are "tribes with flags."

> Libya, Iraq, Jordan, Saudi Arabia, Syria, Bahrain, Yemen, Kuwait, Qatar, and the United Arab Emirates are countries that never melded into a unified family of citizens. The tribes and sects that make up these more artificial states have long been held together by the iron fist of colonial powers, kings or military dictators. They have no real "citizens" in the modern sense. Democratic rotations of power are impossible because each tribe lives by the motto "rule or die"—either my tribe or sect is in power or we're dead.[18]

8. The culture suffers from lack of self-examination and the worship of conspiracy theories. The concept or practice of self-criticism or self-evaluation is absent from the wider Arab discourse. The cultural narrative is rarely open to admitting short-sightedness, misjudgement or plain error. Endless excuses, pointless blaming of anybody but self, family, or tribe is the norm. It is always the outsiders, the devils in many forms, the superstitious

bad luck or curse. Arab people take no responsibility for their choices or judgement. There is no appraisal of the past: what went wrong and how we can do better. This bewildering cycle of belief in conspiracies and lack of self-examination has been the trend since the demise of the Arab empire centuries ago. When reason sleeps, monsters awake.

9. Arab culture is marked by fatalism and religious mythology. Too often one hears Arab people utter the words, “It is in God’s hands” or “That is our fate and destiny.” Surrendering to transcendent powers and unseen forces is taken to the extreme, as if they are the ultimate explanation of reality, existence, and political forces. In such a mind-set, there is no need for scientific research or inquiry. This is why every Arabic-speaking country is behind in scientific discovery and patent registration.

10. Rhetoric and speechmaking re regarded as a substitute for real results or achievement. Poetry is a mesmerizing force in Arab culture. Poets are revered and considered cultural icons. They forget they are in the business of entertainment, sophistry and language manipulation for the sake of an artistic end, no more and no less. For too many people in the Arab world, the study of literature and poetry, theology, and philosophy are producing generations of youth who are unable to find work, be productive, and contribute to their societies and to the world at large. Hence, there is total dependency on importing all technological and scientific discoveries from the West, including all current high-tech gadgets and information technology know-how.

11. The Arab world is typified by a lack of reading, writing, and rationality. One of the main undisputed characteristics of a successful culture is the culture of reading in all its facets. The Arab world falls behind miserably on this score. Consider the following chart and survey. Not

that Ksibi's surveys only looked at nine out of the twenty-two Arab states and counted reading activity in English and French as well as Arabic. But giving this research the benefit of the doubt, here's an interesting glimpse into what Arab readers are like, excerpted from Ksibi's presentation:

Topics Enjoyed by Arab Readers

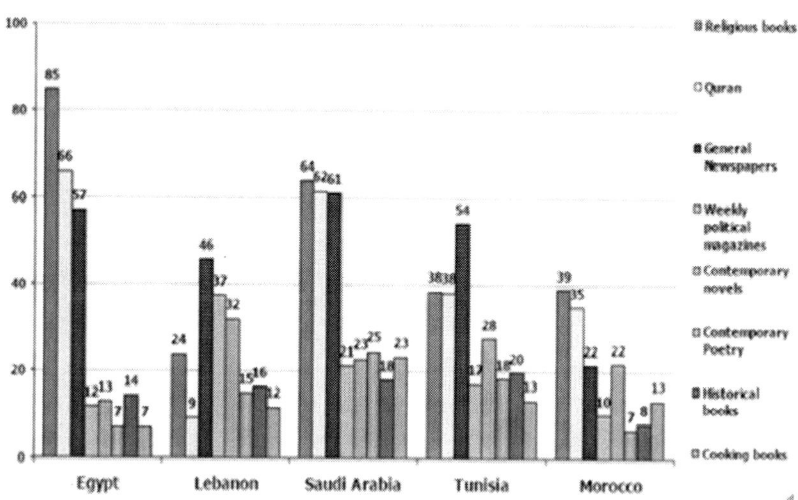

Among the literate population, the highest number of readers is in Egypt and Saudi Arabia (eighty-eight percent and ninety-four percent respectively).[19]

On the other hand, a 2008 UN survey, likely more geographically exhaustive in scope and including illiterate Arabs this time, comes to a far more depressing conclusion: *The average person in the Arab world reads no more than four pages a year*. Americans, contrast, read an average of eleven *books* a year.[20]

No matter who is closer to the truth, both surveys point to the scarcity of book printing in the Arab world to explain why Arabs don't read nearly as much as they should. I'd add to that a decline in the popular and practical use of written

Arabic as a factor. Ksibi conjectures that an illiterate mother can also have an adverse effect on the reading habits of her literate children. These are some of the reasons literate Arabs aren't voracious readers.[21]

The list is long and exhausting. We shall deal with many other aspects of this cultural crash in the chapters ahead. However, it fitting to recall here the words of the great scholar of the Middle East Bernard Lewis:

To a Western observer, schooled in the theory and practice of Western freedom, it is precisely the lack of freedom—freedom of the mind from constraint and indoctrination, to question and inquire and speak; freedom of the economy from corrupt and pervasive mismanagement; freedom of women from male oppression; freedom of citizens from tyranny—that underlines so many of the troubles of the Muslim world. But the road to democracy, as the Western experience amply demonstrates, is long and hard, full of pitfalls and obstacles."[22]

In the following chapter, we will examine the interplay and inter-connectedness between culture and politics and delve into the root causes of the Arabic cultural struggle.

Chapter 2.

It's the Culture, Stupid! The German Model: An Example

The central conservative truth is that it is culture, not politics that determines the success of a society. The central liberal truth is that politics can change a culture and save it from itself.

—Daniel Patrick Moynihan

This city is what it is because our citizens are what they are.

—Plato

The triumph of culture in the Arab Middle East region is now complete. The central conservative cultural truth has won the battle across the Arab political landscape.

The cultural forces that engulf societies, the way of life that shapes us, that builds or retards us, that moulds and refines us, are coalescing into an unstoppable force in most Arab countries, making it clear from one corner to another that what matters most are the cultural packages that people carry from the past into the present on their way into the future.

"Mohamed Bouazizi was the young man who, by setting himself on fire in Sidi Bouzid, a city in central Tunisia, on 17 December 2010, triggered the revolutionary process that would spread to the whole Arabic-speaking region in the space of a few months."[23] The entire Arab political state system collapsed like a house of cards. The common and shared values that existed in most Arab societies manifested themselves in successive uprisings, revolutions, and mini-revolutions or civil strife and chaos. It is evident that the common characteristics of Arab culture, such as language, religion, women's place in society, sexual attitudes, political oppression and state tyranny, totalitarianism, social norms and habits, tradition, and historical myths and attitudes toward modernity, stand in uniformity to a considerable degree and are shared across borders. Culture rules. Culture is supreme. Culture is destiny.

The Roots of the Arab World's Culture Crash

By its very nature, culture is not static or frozen in time. At one period in history, the Arab world was the leading global force of civilization on all levels. To anyone familiar with the Golden Age, which spanned the eighth through the thirteenth centuries of the common era, the disparity between the intellectual achievements of the Middle East then and now—particularly relative to the rest of the world—is staggering. In his 2002 book *What Went Wrong?,* historian Bernard Lewis notes that "for many centuries the world of Islam was in the forefront of human civilization and achievements."[24] Jamil Ragep agrees, noting that, "Nothing in Europe could hold a candle to what was going on in the Islamic world until 1600.

Algebra, algorithm, alchemy, alcohol, alkali, nadir, zenith, coffee, and lemon: these words all derive from Arabic, reflecting Islam's contribution to the West."[25] Therefore, the question is: What went wrong? What happened to that glorious civilization that gave humanity so much for so long?

Here are some shocking modern statistics to put things into perspective:

- Muslim countries have nine scientists, engineers, and technicians per thousand people, compared with a world average of forty-one. In these nations, there are approximately 1,800 universities, but only 312 of those universities have scholars who have published journal articles.
- There are roughly 1.6 billion Muslims in the world, but only two scientists from Muslim countries have won Nobel Prizes in science (one for physics in 1979, the other for chemistry in 1999).
- Forty-six Muslim countries combined contribute just one percent of the world's scientific literature, Spain and India each contribute more of the world's scientific literature than all of those countries taken together.
- Although Spain is hardly an intellectual superpower, it translates more books in a single year than the entire Arab world has in the past one thousand years.
- Arabs comprise 5 percent of the world's population but publish just 1.1 percent of its books, according to the UN's 2003 Arab Human Development Report. Between 1980 and 2000, South Korea granted 16,328 patents, while nine Arab countries, including Egypt, Saudi Arabia, and the UAE, granted a combined total of only 370, many of them registered by foreigners.
- A study in 1989 found that in one year, the United States published 10,481 scientific papers that were frequently cited, while the entire Arab world published only four.

- This may sound like the punchline of a bad joke, but when *Nature* magazine published a sketch of science in the Arab world in 2002, its reporter identified just three scientific areas in which Islamic countries excel: desalination, falconry, and camel reproduction

(Source: http://www.thenewatlantis.com/publications/why-the-arabic-world-turned-away-from-science)

To understand this, a brief historical background is in order. The dynamic and unprecedented empire that the Arabs built from 750 to 1258 ad under the Umayyad caliphs—who ruled in Damascus from 661 to 750—and under the Islamic empire under the Abbasid caliphs—who ruling in Baghdad from 751 to 1258—witnessed the most intellectually productive age in Arab history. Those glory centuries were in sharp contrast to the relatively backward Europe and much of the rest of the world. "Baghdad in particular, the Abbasid capital, was home to palaces, mosques, joint-stock companies, banks, schools, and hospitals; by the tenth century, it was the largest city in the world."[26]

The rise and fall of empires and kingdoms is the rule rather than the exception throughout world history. Over-expansion, insurrections, fragmentation, and provincial autonomy are some of the causes of the collapse of the Abbasid era. Furthermore, two competing schools of thought were at war to win the hearts and minds of the Arab population at that crucial time. The first was the Mu'tazilism, which was influenced by the Greek rationalism of Aristotle. The second was the rise of the anti-rationalist Ash'ari school of thought.

> The beginning of the de-Hellenization of Arabic high culture was under way. By the twelfth or thirteenth century, the influence of the Mu'tazilism was nearly completely marginalized. In fact, its demise was to some measure due to the inquisition that Abbasid caliph Al-Mamun conducted where he

> persecuted those who refused the principles of the Mu'tazilism school of thought by punishing them with flogging, imprisonment or beheading. That created a public backlash and contributed to its eventual demise. In its place arose the anti-rationalist Ash'ari school whose increasing dominance is linked to the decline of Arabic science. With the rise of the Ash'arites, the ethos in the Islamic world was increasingly opposed to original scholarship and any scientific inquiry that did not directly aid in religious regulation of private and public life. While the Mu'tazilites had contended that the Koran was *created* and so God's purpose for man must be interpreted through reason, the Ash'arites believed the Koran to be coeval with God—and therefore unchallengeable.[27]

Put simply, the battle of ideas between these two schools of thought, i.e., the rationalists and the anti-rationalists, and the subsequent victory of the latter determined, to a great degree, the fate of the Arab civilization then and has continued to influence it to this very day. The Arab world is still suffering from the outcome of that battle, the aftershocks of that earthquake still being felt daily in the lives of millions.

Hillel Ofek, in the extraordinary essay cited above, offers this analysis of the enduring effects of the anti-rationalism on Arabic-Islamic narrative and culture in modern times.

> The Ash'ari view has endured to this day. Its most extreme form can be seen in some sects of Islamists. For example, Mohammed Yusuf, the late leader of a group called the Nigerian Taliban, explained why 'Western education is a sin' by explaining its view on rain: "We believe it is a creation of God rather than an evaporation caused by the sun that condenses

> and becomes rain." The Ash'ari view is also evident when Islamic leaders attribute natural disasters to God's vengeance, as they did when they said that the 2010 eruption of Iceland's Eyjafjallajökull volcano was the result of God's anger at immodestly dressed women in Europe. Such inferences sound crazy to Western ears, but given their frequency in the Muslim world, they must sound at least a little less crazy to Muslims. As Robert R. Reilly argues in *The Closing of the Muslim Mind* (2010), "The fatal disconnect between the creator and the mind of his creature is the source of Sunni Islam's most profound woes."[28]

In practical terms, it meant that Islam and Christianity went their separate ways, each claiming to uphold and possess the truth. Science and modernity flourished in Christian Europe while scientific inquiry and progress all but vanished in Arab lands. Moreover, the role of religion became the biggest issue of all.

> Christianity acknowledges a private-public distinction and (theoretically, at least) allows adherents the liberty to decide much about their social and political lives. Islam, on the other hand, denies any private-public distinction and includes laws regulating the most minute details of private life. Put another way, Islam does not acknowledges any difference between religious and political ends: it is a religion that specifies political rules for the community.[29]

This is why, as Bernard Lewis notes in his book *Islam and the West* (1993), "The Renaissance, the Reformation, even the scientific revolution and the Enlightenment, passed unnoticed in the Muslim world."

In summary, the dissolution of the Golden Age of the Arabic-Islamic culture, and the decline of its scientific knowledge and research, were due to the following factors:

1. The fragmentation and factionalization of the Abbasid dynasty. This was followed by the ascendency of the anti-rationalist movement, i.e., the anti-philosophical school known as the Ash'arism, in contrast to the decline of the Greek rationalist school, known as the Mu'tazilism, with its emphasis on Aristotelian logic. This, in turn, produced a belief in divine doctrines and the marginalization of pure reason and scientific inquiry. It also effectively ended the *ijtihad*—independent judgment and critical thinking—by the twelfth century.

   The Church's acceptance and even encouragement of philosophy and science was evident from the High Middle Ages to modern times. On the contrary, Islam closed the gates of scientific studies. Rational disciplines were not institutionalized in classical Islam, and the adoption of Greek legacy had no lasting effect on Islamic civilization.

   The rise of modern science is the result of the development of a culture that is uniquely humanistic in the sense that it tolerates, indeed, protects and promotes these "heretical" and innovative ideas that run counter to accepted religious and theological teaching. Conversely, one might say that critical elements of the scientific worldview were surreptitiously encoded in the religious and legal presuppositions of the European West. (Toby E. Huff's quote from *The Rise of Early Modern Science.)* In other words, Islamic civilization did not have a culture hospitable to the advancement of science while medieval Europe did.

2. The denial of private-public discourse in Arabic-Islamic thought and practice and the mixing of the religious and political realms as inseparable. This means that, for Islam, religion and politics were interdependent from

the beginning. Islam needs a state to enforce its laws, and the state needs a basis in Islam to be legitimate. (The prime example in modern times is Saudi Arabia.)

3. A formal education system with a religious curriculum that emphasizes repetition, drill, imitation, and memorization and discourages questioning and critical or innovative thinking. The third Arab Human Development Report (2005), issued by the UN and written by Arab social scientists, emphasized this point, stating that,

> The family, the primary unit of Arab society, is based on clannism, which implants submission, and is considered the enemy of personal independence, intellectual daring and the flowering of a unique and authentic human entity. Once children enter school, they find an educational institution, curricula, teaching and evaluation methods which tend to rely on dictation and instill submissiveness. This learning environment ...does not open the doors to freedom of thought and criticism.[30]

In contrast, European universities were legally autonomous. They developed their own rules and scholarly norms and incorporated curiosity, skepticism, and innovation. None of that was present in the Arab world. Tellingly, the printing press was not introduced into the Arabic-Islamic world until 1727. Meanwhile, it had been in use in Europe for over 250 years.[31]

Culture and the German Model

Now that we have a general understanding of the reasons behind the decline and fall of the Arab Golden Age, let us turn our attention to modern times and present conditions.

The fateful choice taken in the thirteenth century to follow the path of religious dictation and Islamic teachings as the ultimate and only source of human knowledge and practices at the expense of reason—which teaches us to discover, question, innovate, research, and follow the facts wherever they may lead—made all the difference in the development of Arab culture. Today, the issues that the Arab region is confronting politically, socially, economically, religiously, and in all other aspects of daily living are the ongoing aftershocks of that earthquake.

While the Arab world entered a dark age of confusion, stagnation, and total dependency on importing ideas, technology, and know-how in all walks of life as it abandoned scientific inquiry, the West, as historian Niall Ferguson argues in his book *Civilization,* took off and has dominated the world for the past five centuries. He describes the following six "killer apps" that the West developed and which have allowed the West to dominate globally.

1. Competition, in that Europe itself was politically fragmented and that within each monarchy or republic there were multiple competing corporate entities.

2. The Scientific Revolution, in that all the major seventeenth-century breakthroughs in mathematics, astronomy, physics, chemistry and biology happened in Western Europe.

3. The rule of law and representative government, in that an optimal system of social and political order emerged in the English-speaking world, based on private property rights and the representation of property-owners as elected legislatures.

4. Modern medicine, in that nearly all the major nineteenth- and twentieth-century breakthroughs in health care, including the control of tropical diseases, were made by Western Europeans and North Americans.
5. The consumer society, in that the Industrial Revolution took place where there was both a supply of productivity-enhancing technologies and a demand for more, better and cheaper goods, beginning with cotton garments.
6. The work ethic, in that Westerners were the first people in the world to combine more extensive and intensive labour with higher savings rates, permitting sustained capital accumulation.[32]

It is fashionable and tiresome for the Arab world and its citizens to blame their current predicament on Western imperialism, colonialism, Turkish domination for five hundred years, and then on Israel and other problems. The blame game can only go so far, and then reality comes back with a vengeance. The fact remains that it is the absence of all of the abovementioned "killer apps" plus many other factors, such as political tyranny, repression, feeble institutions, sectarianism, the fusion of church/mosque and state, lack of citizenship, economic stagnation and dependency on oil, oppression of women, out-dated educational systems, religious divisions, tribalism, no rule of law, the absence of social contracts to bind societies, lack of respect for diversity, ethnic strife, absence of freedom, and ever-present conspiracy theories, that are responsible for the region's demise.

Germany stands out as a shining example of a country that was totally destroyed during the Second World War, divided into two parts, humiliated, and almost shattered into oblivion. Yet, beyond all expectations and predictions, the German culture survived, flourished, and thrived. Now Germany is a powerhouse in Europe and internationally. The German model is evidence beyond doubt of the value, power, and resiliency of a sound and well-structured culture that can withstand the test of time because of its inherent authenticity and validity.

The following are some basic characteristics of German culture and its secrets for success.[33]

A Planning Culture

- In many respects, Germans can be considered the masters of planning.
- This is a culture that prizes forward thinking and knowing what they will be doing at a specific time on a specific day.
- Careful planning, in one's business and personal life, provides a sense of security.
- Rules and regulations allow people to know what is expected so that they can plan their life accordingly.
- Germans believe that maintaining clear lines of demarcation between people, places, and things is the surest way to lead a structured and ordered life.
- Work and personal lives are rigidly divided.
- There is a proper time for every activity. When the business day ends, you are expected to leave the office. If you must remain after normal closing, it indicates that you did not plan your day properly.

Education

Getting a good education is very important in German society. Not only do Germans have a deep respect for education, credibility, social status, and the level of employment a person may reach depends on his or her educational achievement. The Germans take great pride in their educational system, especially in the fields of craftsmanship and technology. They also value the Enlightenment concept of the separation of church and state. They cherish the scientific way of solving problems by applying rigorous research and practical application of reason and empiricism.

Manners

Good manners are a must in the German culture. Displaying politeness and courtesy are ways of showing respect. Boundaries are drawn through social distance, eye contact, touch, and facial expressions. Different types of relationships require different codes of behavior. Failing to follow these protocols is considered rude and may alienate those who are unaware of them.

Punctuality

Especially in a business setting, Germans pride themselves on their punctuality. To many of them, being on time is not just a simple concern, it is an obsession. Being late to an appointment disturbs their sense of order and is seen as rude; if you are expecting to be late, call and explain your situation. The German sense of "keeping to the schedule" can be seen in and out of the business world. For those who are virtually always on time, there are rarely acceptable excuses for tardiness or delays that may disturb the "schedule."[34]

Therefore, if Germany can recover from the decimation and humiliation inflicted upon it as a consequences of losing not one but two world wars, there is no reason why the Arab world cannot follow suit. It's all a matter of changing the mind-set, the traditional dependency on religious discourse and thus changing the cultural narrative.

In the following chapters, I will examine the ills that afflict Arab culture as the echo of the anti-rationalist explosive choice taken in the thirteenth century still reverberate in the background of Arab culture. In particular, I will identify the problems of illiteracy, the use and abuse of religious faith, sexuality, women's place in society, economic meltdown, lack of freedom, and the excessive use of rhetoric as a substitute for action and performance as well as other pertinent issues.

Chapter 3.

The Cancer of Illiteracy

The Tunisia-based organization issued a statement on Wednesday to commemorate the Arab Literacy Day stating that "the Human Development Reports for 2013 and the Global Monitoring Report on Education for All for 2012 indicate that among the Arab population which amounted to 353,8 million people, only 256,946 million were familiar with reading and writing, which means that nearly 96,836 million are illiterate. This means that the illiteracy rate in the Arab world has increased to 19.73 percent of the total population, whereas the percentage of female illiterates has amounted to 60.60 percent compared to 39.42 percent male illiterates". However, ALESCO report did include figures from three Arab countries; namely Comoros, Djibouti and Somalia.

(The Arab Organization for Education,
Science and Culture (ALECSO))

Illiteracy in modern times is cancerous, especially if it is high among women. Illiterate mothers produce dysfunctional generations who, in turn, produce failed societies and failed states. Illiteracy in modern times is deadly. Unfortunately, a high illiteracy rate is a fact of life in the Arab world today. It contains the seeds of oppression, lost youth, terrorism, disorientation, and generations lacking proper guidance. It impedes development and generates failed states, producing chaos and strife. A closer examination of the dynamics of illiteracy conveys, to a considerable degree, the depth of the developmental problems infecting the Arab political culture. The consequences of illiteracy are incalculable indeed.

The Illiterate Individual

People are the real wealth of a nation.

—The 1990 United Nations Human Development Report

Modernity has no mercy when it comes to people who cannot read, write, or use math or technical instruments. The ruthlessness of the computer age is similar to medieval tyrants: Obey or become obsolete. Perform or perish.

An illiterate person is like an object flying in space without gravity. To be a member of the social contract, to civilization, to the human drama, to the arts and culture, to science and moderity, to living as a human being full of aliveness, zest and potential for growth, one has to be engaged in the process of reading, writing and rationality. To that end, illiteracy is like a body without a soul.

For individuals, illiteracy limits the ability to obtain and digest information that is essential to functioning on a daily basis. It deprives them of meaningful employment, thus producing low income and lower-quality jobs. It also retards personal development. Worse still, illiteracy has the unpleasant tendency to be replicated in the next generation. It tends to produce large families with limited means for supporting them, leading to overpopulation. It also produces isolation, mental health problems, and low self-esteem. Because of illiteracy, we see workplace accidents and low productivity. All in all, it keeps people imprisoned in virtual cages of futility.

The illiterate Arab individual is inherently weak within his tribe, sect, or society at large, given the cultural importance and pre-eminence of the group or the community in which one finds him or herself. Imagine the illiterate individual and his place in society. He is a tool, an instrument to be used and abused and a pariah in his homeland. No dignity, no rights, no presence, and no meaningful existence. Imagine then the lives of the twenty-five percent of the Arab population who labor under this curse.

Development has been defined as "enlarging people's choices." Illiteracy does exactly the opposite. When the mind is closed, politics, social affairs, religion, economics, human rights, and life itself all become prisoners in a mental jail. When reason sleeps, mumbo-jumbo flourishes. Literacy awakens the magic of reason, and only when we reason we are truly alive.

An illiterate person can easily fall prey to a totalitarian system of servitude or to barbaric gangs like ISIS. Illiteracy is also a fertile ground for theocracy and religious extremism, because it takes advantage of people's lack of means to question, debate, argue, or challenge whatever is being presented to them.

Illiteracy and Society

For the community, illiteracy paralyzes a significant segment of society. In the case of the Arab world, that is almost a quarter of the population. In the new global knowledge economy, no state, no society, and no civilization can survive, grow, and flourish if a sizable chunk of its population can't read or write. Illiteracy freezes society in time. The totalitarian system of political power does not mind illiteracy, because it gives it more ammunition to maintain power and control. Organized religion also benefits from an illiterate population, because it makes it easier for such institutions to gain and keep untold resources and a monopoly on many levels.

Moreover, illiteracy makes progress, economic development, and social change almost impossible. A vicious cycle of stagnation and a stale state of affairs is the assured outcome in most cases. That was the end result in most Arab countries for four to five decades throughout the latter half of the twentieth century. Political, social, economic, and cultural decay was the order of the day. Generation after generation, the Arab world witnessed little change in development, and illiteracy was a major cause of that malfunction. "By 2001, almost every part of the world had seen significant political progress—Eastern Europe, Asia, Latin America, even Africa had held many free and fair elections. But the Arab world remained a desert. In 2001, most Arabs had fewer freedoms than they did in 1951."[35]

Cultural decay goes hand in hand with political decay. An illiterate electorate cares little about political freedom and different value systems. It cannot challenge established norms and out-dated ideas effectively or oppose political authoritarianism. The French philosopher Voltaire was correct in saying, "It is hard to free fools from the chains they revere." Survival is of paramount concern. Political rights and democratic ideals are considered a luxury. And when times are tough, luxuries are the first things to go. No wonder, then, that when the spark of the Arab Spring came it was such a passing flicker in most countries. There was not enough oxygen to keep it alight. It was a dead-man-walking phenomenon.

It is bad enough that a quarter of the Arab population is illiterate. Worse is what the literate portion is reading. Studies show the subjects that are of most interest in the Arab world are the following: religious books, daily newspapers, poetry, cooking, historical books, and political commentary. (Read Ahmed Ksibi's research from the Tunisian information studies college institute in chapter one.) Another study I uncovered during my research on the topic of book reading shows that Arab readers have three basic interests: religious books, poetry, and superstitious books on palm-reading, the evil eye, black magic, sorcery, and the like. This surely does not put food on the table, prepare individuals for employment in a competitive marketplace, or help them function in the modern world.

Egypt, the biggest and most important Arab country, has a huge illiteracy problem especially in rural areas. "According to the 2005 *Human Development Report (HDR)* for Egypt, issued jointly by the *UNDR* and the Ministry of Planning and Development, 35 percent of the population cannot read or write, putting Egypt among the top countries in the world in terms of illiteracy. The figure is worse for Egypt's female population, with 45 percent of girls and women over 15 years-old being illiterate."[36] To add insult to injury, many of these girls are not registered with the civil or governmental institutions.

> For other women, trouble starts at birth. Parents, particularly in impoverished rural areas, are often loath to register their daughters with the authorities. Many parents feel that girls—who aren't seen as potential breadwinners—are simply not worth the trouble. "As a result, many girls grow up without being issued birth certificates or identity cards." Technically, these girls and women do not exist. They are therefore not only unable to attend school, but it also becomes impossible for them to access

public health services and other government subsidies or apply for regular work.[37]

Illiteracy produces two evil results: poor citizens and weak citizens. Nothing short of a cultural revolution is needed to escape this black hole. "'This is going to be a long struggle on many fronts. And it requires a big shift in thinking in the Arab-Muslim world,' argues Husain Haqqani, the former Pakistani ambassador to the U.S., from 'us versus them to us versus our own problems,' and from 'we are weak and poor because we were colonized ' to 'we were colonized because we were weak and poor.'"[38]

Table 1: Adult and youth literacy rates, 2010[39]

Region	Adult literacy rate (%)			Youth literacy rate (%)		
	Total	Male	Female	Total	Male	Female
Arab States	74.7	83.3	65.7	89.1	92.4	85.6
Central Asia	99.5	99.6	99.4	99.7	99.6	99.8
Central and Eastern Europe	97.9	99.0	97.0	99.1	99.3	98.9
East Asia and the Pacific	94.2	96.7	91.6	98.8	98.9	98.7
Latin America and the Caribbean	91.4	92.1	90.7	97.2	97.0	97.4
North America and Western Europe	-	-	-	-	-	-
South and West Asia	62.7	74.0	51.8	80.5	86.6	74.7
Sub-Saharan Africa	62.6	71.0	54.2	71.8	76.4	66.8
World	84.1	88.6	79.7	89.6	92.2	87.1

Pierre Tristam, Middle East Issues Expert

Adult Illiteracy Rates (15 Years and Over) in the Middle East

Some 774 million adults worldwide (ages fifteen and over) can't read.[40] Here's how the Middle East countries' illiteracy rates rank.

Middle East Illiteracy Rates

Rank	Country	Illiteracy rate (%)	Rank	Country	Illiteracy rate (%)
1	Afghanistan	72	16	Saudi Arabia	17.1
2	Pakistan	50	17	Libya	16
3	Mauritania	49	18	Bahrain	13
4	Morocco	48	19	Turkey	12.6
5	Yemen	46	20	Lebanon	12
6	Sudan	39	21	U.A.E.	11.3
7	Djibouti	32	22	Qatar	11
8	Algeria	30	23	Jordan	9
9	Iraq	26	24	Palestine	8
10	Tunisia	25.7	25	Kuwait	7
11	Egypt	28	26	Cyprus	3.2
12	Comoros	25	27	Israel	3
13	Syria	19	28	Azerbaijan	1.2
14	Oman	18	29	Armenia	1
15	Iran	17.6			

Sources: United Nations, 2009 World Almanac, The Economist

Illiteracy is not the only factor negatively affecting Arab cultural crisis or state of affairs as they exist these days. But, undoubtedly, it is a contributing element for Arab predicament. Modernity with its empahsis on the knowledge-based economies, on innovation, economic growth and entrepreneurial talent and constant adaptation to changing social, political and economic realities, depends, to a large degree, on a literate population with the tools to succeed.

With the rates of illiteracy in the Arab countries, especially amony women, as the abovementioned numbers indicate, the future is nothing short of a depressing challenge. A massive educational campaign must be launched to compat this cancer.

Illiteracy is one of many challenges facing Arab culture and its fight with modernity as we shall discover in the following chapters.

Chapter 4.

Religion Used and Abused: Fighting Over Heaven and Losing Earth

Religion is part of the human make-up. It's also part of our cultural and intellectual history. Religion was our first attempt at literature, the texts, our first attempt at cosmology, making sense of where we are in the universe, our first attempt at health care, believing in faith healing, our first attempt at philosophy.

—Christopher Hitchens

Both Judaism and Christianity have made progress over the centuries in weeding out dualism—reinterpreting their violent scriptural texts and finding resources of "respect for the other." For Christianity, this transition wasn't easy, involving the Reformation and the Thirty Year's War. But this bloody, chaotic process eventually produced a flowering of powerful ideas in the 17th century: the social contract, human rights and liberty of conscience."

—Michael Gerson, The violent narrative of religious rivalry, *The Washington Post*, May 11, 2015

Religion in the Arab world is not just about identity, belief system, or an instrument used for solidarity and social cohesion. Neither is it a response to states' or societies' failure to deliver services in modern times. It is viewed as the only prism through which one ought to view the world and our place in it. One's religion, sect, or affiliation is a window that colors one's station and understanding of time and place. "What both believers and the critics often miss," writes author Reza Aslan, "is that religion is often far more a matter of identity than it is a matter of beliefs and practices. The phrase 'I am a Muslim,' 'I am a Christian,' 'I am a Jew' and the like is, often, not so much a description of what a person believes or what rituals he or she follows, as a simple statement of identity, of how the speaker views her or his place in the world."[41] This may be true in many cultures around the world, but the exceptionalism of the Arab world in this regard is striking, to say the least. It is, in fact, the continuation of the anti-rationalist inclination since the thirteenth century.

I was born in a place where the dominance of religious narrative and competing faith systems are a prime example of the total cultural hegemony of religion over society. Lebanon, my birthplace, is a country where organized religion was, and still is, the substitute for air, water, food, and the social contract. In fact, the "Lebanonization" of the Arab world is now a given. Look at Syria, Iraq, Yemen, Libya, and other Middle Eastern states, and you will discover that religious divisions run deep, and most social, political, and even economic issues are colored and dominated by religious discourse. Few places on Earth resemble the Arab world, where a person is indoctrinated with a religious narrative as soon as he or she is born. A person's identity, social status, employment, marriage, education, indeed, his or her very future and most of his or her decisions in life are controlled by the religious sect into which the person was born or the environment in which he or she happens to be living. Nothing escapes the gravity of the religious pull in that part of the world. It is an ultimate man-made black hole of cosmic proportions.

Lebanon has always been described as the microcosm of the Arab world. It is considered a bridge between East and West and as an experiment in religious co-existence under one political roof. It is the only country where Christains and Muslims share power and live together, with many problems and strife, of course, yet it functions as a model or as a laboratory for the Arab world. My experience during the "Lebanese War" from (1975–1980) taught me one basic lesson: There is no relationship between religious beliefs and moral action or practice during times of war and upheaval. Lebanon has eighteen officially recognized religious sects, each eyeing the other at all times, with tensions simmering just below the surface. God is on *our* side. A virtual contract binds us together to the exclusion of other tribes. Your religion is not the real one, and on and on it goes. Neighbors who were having dinners and coffee together just a few weeks earlier turned on each other like savages when a particular religious or political leader was assassinated or a different kidnapping occurred the day before.

Syria, Iraq, Yemen, and Libya are now in the middle stages of the Lebanonization process. Witness the unspeakable horrors of ethnic cleansing, sectarian suicide bombings in places of worship, and Sunni vs. Shia wars in ancient cities in Syria and Iraq, where, ironically, the destruction of historical treasures is celebrated as a victory against the infidels of modernity. Where else on Earth can we find such atrocities? Welcome to the land of the three Abrahamic faiths. Welcome to the past, to the present, and to the future as one bundle at a discount price!

Note: In this regard, I strongly urge the reader to read "So . . . Yalla, dear Lebanon" in order to form a proper and complete understanding of the plight of Lebanon, which is a microcosm of the Arab world. It was written by outgoing British Ambassador to Lebanon Mr. Tom Fletcher and published on February 8, 2015[42].

Religion and the Arab Awakening

> *History has justified the Church in the belief that the masses of mankind desire a religion rich in miracle, mystery, and myth.*
>
> —Will and Ariel Durant

On December 18, 2010, the protests started in Tunisia, ushering the start of the Arab Spring. On January 14, 2011, Zine El Abidine Ben Ali, President of Tunisia, was overthrown and fled into exile to Saudi Arabia. Then the fire spread to Egypt, Libya, Syria, Yemen, Jordan, and other Arab countries and was hailed as a historic opportunity for the Arab people to take charge of their lives, start anew, and join the march into modernity. But as the Roman historian Tacitus once remarked, "The best day after a bad emperor is the first."

On the second day, after deposing depots, tyrants, and authoritarian presidents, reality appeared without warning. Totalitarianism left Arab societies like an empty shell devoid of content, of civil society, of institutions, of a public square space, of meaningful civic entities to which the people could turn in situations of need or chaos. When the tyrant was overthrown, the palace vacated, people went straight to the mosque, where they rediscovered their sectarian and tribal roots. From the tyranny of the state and the security services, the people of most countries in the Arab uprisings turned to the tyranny of yesterday, of tradition and tribalism and religious exclusionism. Sunni vs. Shia, Christian vs. Muslim, and Kurd vs. Arab. The list is endless in an ancient territory where so much history was created with so little ability to forget and forgive. We were all "back to the future"!

> There is so much state failures in the Arab world, argues Francis Fukuyama, because of the persistence there of kingship/tribal loyalties—"meaning that you can only trust that narrow group of people in your tribe." You can't build a strong, impersonal, merit-based state when the only ties that bind are shared kin, not shared values. It took China and Europe centuries to make that transition, but they did. If the Arab world can't overcome its tribalism and sectarianism in the face of ISIS barbarism, 'then there is nothing we can do,' said Fukuyama. And theirs will be a future of many dark nights.[43]

ISIS and Abdel Fattah el-Sisi, the new strongman and president of Egypt, are both symptoms of what ails the Arab world.

> ISIS and Sisi, argues Perlov, a researcher on Middle East social networks at Tel Aviv University's Institute for National Security Studies, are just flip sides of the same coin: one elevates "god" as the arbiter of all political life and the other "the national state." . . . Both the secular authoritarian model—most recently represented by Sisi—and the radical religious model—represented now by ISIS—have failed, adds Marwan Muasher, the former foreign minister of Jordan and author of "The Second Arab Awakening and the Battle for Pluralism." They did because they have not addressed people's

> real needs: improving the quality of their life, both in economic and development terms, and also in feeling they are part of the decision-making process. Both models have been exclusionist, presenting themselves as the holders of absolute truth and of the solution to all society's problems.[44]

The images we see today coming from the Arab part of the Middle East are a reminder of what we learned in history books about Europe five hundred years ago. The religious divide between Catholics and Protestants and the sectarian wars that savaged Europe are strikingly similar to the Sunni-Shia sectarian strife in Arab lands. "What's happened, of course, is that the Middle East has begun what Richard Haass of the Council on Foreign Relations has called its 30 Year's War—an overlapping series of clashes and proxy wars that could go on for decades and transform identities, maps and the political contours of the region."[45]

In light of this, the central question is, what has been holding back the Arab world since the end of the thirteenth century? In my opinion, there are two fundamental causes: First, the continuation of the anti-rationalist tradition that we discussed in chapter two, along with the perpetuation of the conservative and orthodox interpretations of the religious texts to appease the extreme elements of the religious establishment. Saudi Arabia, Egypt, and Yemen are prime examples. Second, the totalitarian system of the political order and its monopoly, corruption, abuse of power, and suffocation of diversity, all coalesced to create a perfect storm that started at the end of 2010 until today.

> Egypt's striking lesson today is that its two powerful, organized and trusted groups—the Muslim Brotherhood and the armed forces—both proved to be incompetent in the business of governance, the political scientist Rami Khouri

wrote in the *Beirut Daily Star* last week. This is not because they do not have capable individuals and smart and rational supporters; they have plenty of those. It is rather because the ways of soldiers and spirituality are designed for worlds other than governance and equitably providing services and opportunities for millions of people from different religions, ideologies and ethnicities . . . The lack of other organized and credible indigenous groups of citizens that can engage in the political process and shape new constitutional systems is largely a consequences of how military officers, members of tribes, and religious zealots have dominated Arab public life for decades.[46]

Fighting Over Heaven, Losing Earth

Whatever one's beliefs, secular or religious, there should be complete freedom to express them, short of inciting violence. Whatever one's beliefs, there should be freedom to assemble to promote them. And whatever one's beliefs, there should be freedom to act upon those beliefs, so long as, in so doing, one neither physically harms another individual nor transgresses that individual's right in the public sphere. These should be the fundamental principles by which we judge the permissibility of any belief or act, religious or secular.

—Kenan Malik, in the New York Times, January 12, 2014

The primacy of religion in the Arab world is no small matter. It controls the cultural landscape from one end to the other. It defines every aspect of life. It is the oxygen of Arab culture. This oxygen often helped the poor through hope. It offered solace to the bereaved, the old, the unlucky, and the unhappy. It offered supernatural comfort to millions of miserable souls suffering under torture, tyranny, and totalitarianism.

However, religion has been used, and is being used, in the Arab world by the state, mostly despotic, to further its control over the masses. A tacit contract has been established between the authoritarian regimes and the religious establishment to divide the pie and extend a helping hand to each other, obstructing social change, liberal policies, and democratic development. Saudi Arabia's royal family's contract with the ultra-conservative Wahabbi version of Islam is a prime example. The governing royal family gets its legitimacy from the Islamic establishment in exchange for adhering to its orthodoxy and conservative notions and interpretations of Islam. In Syria, the regime succeeded in playing the religious card for many years until the advent of the Arab Spring in 2011. In Egypt, the Christian minority was persecuted to appease the religious establishment. The same formula worked just as well in Europe centuries ago.

> The irreligion of eighteenth-century England disappeared under the Victorian compromise with Christianity: the state agreed to support the Anglican Church, and the educated classes would muffle their skepticism, on the tacit understanding that the Church would accept subordination to the state, and the parson would humbly serve the squire. In America the rationalism of the Founding Fathers gave place to a religious revival in the nineteenth century.[47]

Now the absence of any notion of the separation of mosque/church and state/politics in the wider Arab culture has created a combustible mixture of religious powder that has resulted in a renewed civil war between Sunni and Shia sects, between Christian minorities and Muslim majorities, and led to the persecution and slaughter of other religious minorities scattered across the Arab lands. (Witness the ethnic cleansing and killings of the Yazidis in Iraq and other minorities in Syria at the hands of ISIS in 2014.)

Professor Ahmad F. Yousif, from the International Islamic University of Malaysia, wrote about the Islamic perspective of religious freedom, arguing that,

> The concept of separation between sacred and profane, or religious and secular, is completely non-existent in Islam, which is based on the recognition of the unity of the Creator and the submission of the individual's will to Him. Furthermore, Islam is not a religion in the Western sense of the word, confining its scope to the private life of the individual, but instead, "provides guidance for all walks of life—Individual and social, material and moral, economic and political, legal and cultural, national and international."[48]

Dr. Yousif goes on to argue that comparing the Western system and the Islamic system in terms of religion's role in society is like comparing apples to oranges.

> As we have seen, the liberal democratic state considers religion for the most part as a personal, private matter, just one of many spheres of life and distinct from the more important "rational" aspects of life. Conversely, from the Islamic perspective, religion is viewed as an integrated whole. As the individual submits his/her will to the will of God and carries out activities for the sake of God, all aspects of

> life become spiritualized and indeed acts of worship.[49]

It is instructive to note that the period of the Protestant Reformation, which took place in Europe from 1517–1648, was the main reason behind the rise of the West. It produced the formula of separation of church and state, which worked better than anything tried before. And this was after years of religious wars, misery, persecution, and sectarian mayhem. "In Europe, this reality was reinforced by the Treaty of Westphalia in 1648, which essentially privatized religion to the realm of individual belief and nationalized it as the basis for organizing modern states."[50]

Simply put, the Arab world needs its own reformation, its own version of the Westphalia treaty, and it needs to get to work on this as soon as possible, because the march of history never stops. The rise of the rest is leaving the Arab world well behind. The caravan of history moves on.

Religion, Faith, and the Five Lessons of Spirituality

To stop fighting over Heaven and losing Earth, the Arab world needs to take a serious look at how it views religion and its place in the private and public spheres. It needs to re-examine the traditional assumptions of what it means to be religious and that for which faith stands. Sally Quinn, in her summation essay regarding the lessons she learned from the "On Faith" series in *The Washington Post*, wrote the following five lessons learned as a distillation of the faith question:

> 1. *Nobody Knows:* "My favorite bumper sticker and the guiding wisdom for me every day is this: 'I don't know and you don't either.'"

2. *All Religions Are The Same—And Not:* "The differences, though, are in the expressions and traditions of each faith. I still believe, despite all of the arguments, that all religions were founded on the notion of community." The Confucius's Golden Rule is universal.

3. *Everything Is About Religion:* Marriage, abortion, homosexuality, poverty, separation of church and state, education, children, books, women's rights, racism, families, medicine, science, crime and punishment, environment, sexual abuse, war and peace and on and on.

4. *We Are All Looking For Meaning:* "Life is hard. No matter whether you are religious or not, you will have periods of extreme doubt which will make you ask, 'What is the point?'" The search for meaning is the greatest human conversation. It cannot get bigger or more serious than this subject.

5. *Why There is Suffering:* "How do you explain suffering?" "How could a loving, all-powerful God allow suffering?" Some of the greatest theologians I have met will simply throw up their hands and admit that they don't understand it either.

Once religion and faith are understood and practiced within the confines of history and with tolerance of other points of view and other faiths, then peace is possible. The Arab world simple cannot keep fighting over Heaven, however defined, and lose the battle for Earth.

Chapter 5.

Women in the Arab World: The Insignificant Others!

Not a single Arab country ranks in the top 100 in the World Economic Forum's Global Gender Gap Report, putting the region as a whole solidly at the planet's rock bottom. Poor or rich, we all hate our women. Neighbors Saudi Arabia and Yemen, for instance, might be eons apart when it comes to GDP, but only four places separate them on the index, with the kingdom at 131 and Yemen coming in at 135 out of 135 countries.

—Mona Eltahawy in "Why Do They Hate Us?" in Foreign Policy magazine

The issue of the veil then became the incentive behind Annas Barakat's decision to pursue medicine and become the first woman doctor in the Arab world. She took the decision after hearing a conservative friend of hers claim that she would leave her sick mother to die rather than incur the shame of asking a male doctor to treat her.

—American University of Beirut Bulletin reporting on Emily Nasrallah's lecture on pioneer Arab women January 18, 2005

"Confessions" is the story of an educated, middle-class Egyptian woman struggling for equality in a man's world. In school, at home and in the office she is caught in "the constant struggle between the thirst for love and fear of men."

—The New York Times, September 13, 1964.

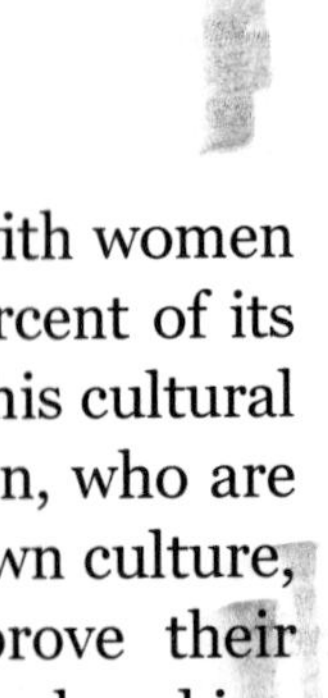

The Arab world has a phenomenal problem with women and sexuality. Why is it that almost fifty percent of its population is virtually invisible? What is behind this cultural catastrophe? What is the matter with Arab women, who are still taking it on the chin, made pariahs in their own culture, and made impotent to effect change and improve their standing while other women all over the world are breaking through barriers of all kinds? What is wrong with the cultural and religious forces in the Arab world as far as women are concerned? Most importantly, what can be done?

Women in Arab Lands: Some Striking Statistics

The following picture offered by gender experts and conducted by Thomson Reuters in August and September of 2013 shows how women's rights in the Arab world are at a catastrophic state compared to the rest of the globe. When fifty percent of the population is in such a state, no wonder we are witnessing the calamitous collapse of most Arab state systems and venomous sectarian, social, and sadistic outcomes. The survey covers twenty-two Arab countries, but I have selected only some according to their population and geopolitical importance for the region.[51]

> Egypt is the worst country for women in the Arab world, closely followed by Iraq, Saudi Arabia, Syria and Yemen, according to gender experts surveyed in a Thomson Reuters Foundation poll released on Tuesday.
>
> Comoros, Oman, Kuwait, Jordan and Qatar came at the top of the survey, which assessed 22 Arab states on violence against women, reproductive rights, treatment of women within the family, their integration into society and attitudes towards a woman's role in politics and the economy.
>
> The results were drawn from answers from 336 gender experts invited to participate in an online survey by the philanthropic arm of the news and information company Thomson Reuters, in August and September of 2013.
>
> Questions were based on key provisions of the U.N. Convention to Eliminate All Forms of Discrimination Against Women (CEDAW), which 19 Arab states have signed or ratified.
>
> The poll assessed violence against women, reproductive rights, treatment of women within the family, their integration into society and

attitudes towards a woman's role in politics and the economy.

Experts were asked to respond to statements and rate the importance of factors affecting women's rights across the six categories. Their responses were converted into scores, which were averaged to create a ranking.

Here are key facts on women's rights in the 22 states surveyed, listed from worst to best."

22. EGYPT

Sexual violence, harassment and trafficking combined with a breakdown of security, high rates of female genital mutilation and a rollback of freedoms since the 2011 revolution put Egypt at the bottom of the poll.

* 99.3 percent of women and girls are subjected to sexual harassment.

* 27.2 million women and girls — or 91 percent of the female population — are victims of female genital mutilation (FGM).

* 63 percent of adult women are literate.

(Sources: U.N. Women, UNICEF, World Bank)

21. IRAQ

Iraq's second-worst ranking reflects a dramatic deterioration in conditions for women since the 2003 U.S.-led invasion. Mass displacement has made women vulnerable to trafficking and sexual violence. The Iraqi penal code allows men who kill their wives to serve a maximum of three years in prison rather than a life sentence.

* 14.5 percent of women have jobs.

* 1.6 million women are widows.

* Thousands of displaced women have been forced to work as prostitutes in neighboring countries including Syria, Jordan and United Arab Emirates.

(Sources: World Bank, Refugees International, Freedom House)

20. SAUDI ARABIA

Saudi Arabia polled third-worst overall and ranked last for political representation and inheritance rights. Despite stirrings of progress, the kingdom's guardianship system severely limits women's freedoms.

* Women can vote for the first time in 2015 municipal elections.

* Marital rape is not recognized and rape victims risk being charged with adultery.

* Women are banned from driving and need a guardian's permission to travel, enroll in education, marry or undergo healthcare procedures.

(Sources: Human Rights Watch, U.S. State Department, Amnesty International)

19. SYRIA

Massive war displacement, both inside Syria and across borders, has left millions of women and girls vulnerable to sexual violence and trafficking, the United Nations says. The collapse of the economy and healthcare system has disproportionately affected women.

* Girls as young as 12 have been married in refugee camps.

* More than 4,000 cases of rape and sexual mutilation have been reported to the Syrian Network for Human Rights.

* There are reports of government forces and armed militias sexually abusing women and girls during home raids and in detention centers.

(UNICEF, U.S. State Department, Human Rights Watch)

18. YEMEN

Historically marginalized, Yemeni women have been fighting for rights since the 2011 Arab Spring. Experts say child marriage, human trafficking and rape are endemic.

* No law deals effectively with domestic abuse and marital rape isn't recognized.

* There is no legal minimum age for marriage.

* 53 percent of girls finish primary school.

(Sources: UNICEF, U.S. State Department, World Bank)

17. SUDAN

Sudan hasn't ratified CEDAW and women face systematic discrimination and inequality. Strict interpretations of Islam curb women's freedoms and allow domestic abuse, child marriage and marital rape. Sexual violence is common and often goes unpunished.

* Girls can legally marry from the age of 10.

* 12.1 million women and girls are victims of FGM.

* Victims often don't report rape, fearing they will be tried for adultery.

(Sources: UNICEF, OECD Gender Index)

16. LEBANON

Lebanon ranked badly for not punishing marital rape, for biased inheritance laws and discriminatory employment laws.

* No law prohibits sexual harassment in the workplace.

* Lebanese women can't pass citizenship onto children or foreign-born husbands.

* One in six Lebanese women is illiterate.

(Sources: Freedom House, UNICEF, U.S. State Department)

15. PALESTINIAN TERRITORIES

Israeli restrictions on movement have severe consequences for Palestinian women, experts said. Women suffer from poverty, unemployment and a high risk of domestic violence and honor crimes.

* Only 17 percent of women are employed despite a literacy rate of 93 percent.

* 51 percent of women in Gaza City experienced domestic violence in 2011.

* 25 honor killings were recorded in the first nine months of 2013.

(Sources: UNICEF, Palestinian Bureau of Statistics, Ma'an News Agency)

10. UNITED ARAB EMIRATES

Women have access to education and health services but traditional gender roles are ingrained. Many foreign female domestic workers are trafficked and abused and women run the risk of being imprisoned for adultery when reporting sexual violence.

* Marital rape is not recognized and the law permits men to discipline their wives physically.

* Four women sit on the 22-member cabinet of the Federal National Council.

* Women represent 14 percent of the total workforce.

(Sources: Human Rights Watch, U.S. State Department, World Bank)

9. LIBYA

Libya ranked as one of the best countries for political representation but experts said insecurity, poverty and lack of education were some of the greatest concerns for women.

* 33 women were elected to the 200-member General National Congress in 2012.

* 20 is the legal minimum age for women to marry unless they get special permission from a court.

* Intimidation and harassment of women by militias and extremists has been widely reported.

(Sources: U.S. State department, UNICEF)

8. MOROCCO

Women in Morocco have a degree of independence and autonomy but domestic abuse is common. Experts say equality laws are not implemented and there are no laws against domestic violence or marital rape.

* 17,000 incidents of violence against women were reported in the first 3 months of 2008.

* 44 percent of women between the ages of 15 and 49 are literate.

* The Penal Code criminalizes anyone who harbors a woman who has left her husband.

(Sources: Freedom House, World Bank, Human Rights Watch)

7. ALGERIA

Algeria ranked badly for gender discrimination in the workplace and political participation by women.

* Algerian law doesn't recognize spousal rape.

* 16 percent of Algerian women have jobs.

* In October 2012, Algeria made its first-ever conviction for sexual harassment.

(Sources: UNICEF, World Bank, U.S. State Department)

6. TUNISIA

Long known as one of the Arab world's most progressive states, Tunisia has offered abortion on demand since 1965 and women can pass citizenship onto their husbands. Conservative elements are now calling for Islamic values to be enforced.

* In 2011, 61 women were elected to the 217-member Constituent Assembly.

* Women are entitled to 30 days maternity leave at 67 percent of full wages.

* Domestic abuse and marital rape laws are rarely enforced.

(Sources: U.S. State Department,
World Bank, Freedom House)

4. JORDAN

Despite its reputation as a progressive state, Jordan ranked second-worst in the category of honor killings.

* 681 cases of rape and sexual assault were reported to the Family Protection Department in 2012.

* 10 honor crimes were brought before judges in 2012 and 24 women went into protective custody to avoid honor killings.

* In 2003, the law was changed so women could get passports without the consent of husbands.

(Sources: U.S. State Department, UNICEF)

3. KUWAIT

Kuwait scored well on education and inheritance rights, though social protections are rarely extended to the country's large female foreign worker population.

* Kuwait has no laws against domestic abuse and marital rape.

* There are no shelters or hotlines for victims of domestic abuse.

* 15 is the minimum legal age for girls to marry.

(Sources: UNICEF, U.S. State Department)

1. COMOROS

The Indian Ocean archipelago nation polled well across all categories except political representation. Comorian women have a good deal of social freedom while sexual abuse is recognized and punished.

* Women hold only 3 percent of seats in the national parliament.

* 35 percent of adult women have jobs.

* Half the inmates of Moroni prison were jailed for sexual aggression.

(Sources: World Bank, U.N. Development Program, U.S. State Department)

No Women; Lots of Cries

Half a mind, half a creed, half an inheritance.

—Arab proverb

> *This isn't because women are better or nicer than men. It's because women make up half of humanity, and when women are held back, humanity remains enchained.*
>
> —Terry Glavin in *The Ottawa Citizen*

What words, what thoughts, and what statements can one add after reading such a depressingly debilitating and destructive, even deadly, state of affairs for most women in the Arab world? Words are empty of meaning in the face such an overwhelming calamitous cultural disaster that is, in fact, a silent social tsunami at the Arab body politic. The question is: What is holding Arab women back, even when education is on the rise and the interconnectedness of our present world is so prevalent? Again, it's the culture, stupid!

On December 7, 2006, *Time* tackled this very subject after the release of the Arab Human Development Report (AHDR), complied under the auspices of the United Nations Development Fund. The report was entitled "Towards the Rise of Women in the Arab World," and it was written by distinguished Arab thinkers from all walks of life. "The rise of the Arab women, " the report argues, "is in fact a prerequisite for an Arab renaissance and causally linked to the fate of the Arab world and its achievement of human development."[52]

The hopes for an Arab renaissance have turned into an Arab nightmare. The ascendency of savage, medieval-like organizations and barbaric outlaw groups, including the likes of Al Qaeda, ISIS, Boko Haram, and al-Shabaab, groups that worship death and martyrdom and create their own imaginative universes, has refocused the debate on the role of culture, women, and religion in dealing with matters of war and peace. The AHDR report identified four major issues that contribute to the plight of Arab women:

1. Education: "The Arab countries have one of the highest rates of female illiteracy in the world. Lack of education and gender discrimination combine to keep the percentage of employed Arab women at only one-third, the lowest in the world. These conditions contribute to unhealthy lifestyles, resulting in higher rates of diseases and deaths linked to pregnancy and childbirth."[53]

2. The legal system: "Laws often restrict women's personal liberties, for example by giving them lesser status than their husbands in divorce proceedings, and requiring the permission of a husband or father to work, travel or borrow from a bank."[54] This does not mention the horrible suffering that some women face due to so-called "honor killings," which is a cultural/societal shame that still affects many Arab counties and is covered up by the state, organized religion, and family members under a cloak of deadly silence.

3. Patriarchal tradition: "The report traces the predicament of Arab women to the region's longstanding patriarchal traditions of protection and 'honor' wrapped into tribal identity. The authoritarian regimes that emerged with Arab independence a half century ago have undermined liberal institutions and values that might have better encouraged women's rights and protected them under a rule of law."[55]

5. Islamic jurisprudence: "Women's prospects are further weakened by regressive Islamic jurisprudence that effectively codifies discrimination against women. So entrenched has this discrimination become, the report notes, that hundreds of popular Arab proverbs scorn women for having 'half a mind, half a creed, half an inheritance'."[56] The report, furthermore, envisions that for reform to take place, there must be a modernization in interpretation and a new jurisprudence on the part of the religious establishment for an enlightened reading of Koranic texts.

Female Genital Mutilation, Hijab, and Women in the Arab World

When it comes to the horrible subject of female genital mutilation/cutting (FGM/C), it is often argued that this is where culture and religion intersect. Scholars debate, disagree, and discuss papers and literature on the subject while millions of girls suffer in agony and sometimes die during this barbaric practice.

> Among social activists and feminists, combating female genital mutilation (FGM) is an important policy goal. Sometimes called female circumcision or female genital cutting, FGM is the cutting of the clitoris of girls in order to curb their sexual desire and preserves their sexual honor before marriage. . . . New information from Iraqi Kurdistan raises the possibility that the problem is more prevalent in the Middle East than previously believed and that FGM is far more tied to religion than many Western academics and activists admit.[57]

The Role of Religion in the Continuation of FGM/C

> FGM/C is often seen to be somehow connected to Islam, a view that is perhaps unsurprising given the frequency with which it is practised by many Muslim African groups. However, not all Islamic groups practise FGM/C, and many non-Islamic groups do. Gruenbaum has emphasized that followers of all three monotheistic religions—Christianity, Judaism and Islam—"have

> at times practised female circumcision and consider their practices sanctioned, or at least not prohibited, by God."
>
> Despite the fact that FGM/C predates the birth of Islam and Christianity and is not mandated by religious scriptures, the belief that it is a religious requirement contributes to the continuation of the practice in a number of settings. As illustrated in the previous section and confirmed by ethnographic studies, in certain settings FGM/C is widely held to be a religious obligation.
>
> In countries such as Guinea, Mali and Mauritania, significant proportions of women and men reported that FGM/C is required by their religion. This is often closely linked to the response of cleanliness/hygiene, since FGM/C has become understood in some Muslim communities to be a cleansing rite that enables women to pray in a proper manner.[58]

Egypt practices genital mutilation on ninety-one percent of its girls. Somalia has the "honor" of being at almost one hundred percent—actually ninety-eight percent! Sudan stands at eighty-eight percent, and many other Persian Gulf States are in the mid-seventies.[59]

> There are indications that FGM might be a phenomenon of epidemic proportions in the Arab Middle East. . . . Arab governments refuse to address the problem. They prefer to believe that lack of statistics will enable international organizations to conclude that the problem does not exist in their jurisdictions. It is not enough to

> consult Islamic clerics to learn about the mutilation of girls in Islamic societies—that is like asking the cook if the guests like the meal.[60]

It is surreal to even discuss and write about such a problem in the modern age. But, as is apparent, modernity and cultural/religious practices collide in many places, making it difficult to believe we exist on the same planet!

When it comes to headscarves or head coverings, moreover, the Arab world is also at war with modernity. Let us define, if possible, some of the terms used in this debate.

> *Hijab:* The hijab is one name for a variety of similar headscarves . . . These veils consist of one or two scarves that cover the head and neck. Outside the West, this traditional veil is worn by many Muslim women in the Arab world and beyond.
>
> *Niqab:* The niqab covers the entire body, head and face; however, an opening is left for the eyes. The two main styles of niqab are the half-niqab that consists of a headscarf and facial veil that leaves the eyes and part of the forehead visible, and the full, or Gulf, niqab that leaves only a narrow slit for the eyes.
>
> *Chador:* The chador is a full-body-length shawl held closed at the neck by hand or pin. It covers the head and the body but leaves the face completely visible.
>
> *Burqa:* The burqa is a full-body veil. The wearer's entire face and body are covered, and one sees through a mesh screen over the eyes. It is most commonly worn in Afghanistan

> and Pakistan. Under the Taliban regime in Afghanistan (1996–2001), its use was mandated by law.
>
> Again, culture and religion intersect to create this hot debate, mostly useless and harmful, as to what a woman should or shouldn't wear. Most of these styles predate Islam, Christianity or Judaism. Sociologist Caitlin Killian argues that "The veil itself, however, predates Islam and was practiced by women of several religions. It also was largely linked to class position: Wealthy women could afford to veil their bodies completely, whereas poor women who had to work [in the field] either modified their veil or did not wear them at all."[61]

The historical currents are abundantly clear. In both cases—the genital mutilation problem and the issue of head coverings—we can see that cultural forces are intertwined organically with religious establishments and that, over time, they have become impossible to separate or disentangle. The Arab world is deep inside this cultural and religious whirlwind, and it shows.

It shows in how women are harassed and treated daily on the streets in Cairo, Libya, Sudan and other places while the authorities look the other way. It shows in the illiteracy rates among women in Arab lands. It shows in the UN's Arab human development reports published before the Arab revolts. It shows an Arab cultural obsession with control over women's bodies and what is permissible in the private and public domain. It shows in what women are allowed to wear, in what way, in what style, and in what place, as if they have no say in the matter. Women are subjected to total control in the name of deference to authority, piety, and virtue, however it is defined. It shows in the honor killings phenomenon in most Arab countries. It shows in the lack of public participation of women in the fields of politics, law, public institutions, science, political parties, big business, and other positions of authority. It shows in the suffocating forces of religious, political, and social environments where women are treated like second-class citizens. It shows in the press treatment of women's issues where the "Ministry of Information" of authoritarian regimes jail and kill journalists who dare to cover abuses and report stories of harassment that reflect poorly on the government. It shows in the absence of women from public places and how social expectations shape social roles, norms, and behavior. It shows in most cultural forces in most Arab societies, period.

Religion and Women

As soon as we abandon our own reason, and are content to rely upon authority, there is no end to our trouble.

—Bertrand Russell

In December 2009, former US President Jimmy Carter told the Parliament of the World's Religions in Australia the following: "Women are prevented from playing a full and equal role in many faiths, creating an environment in which violations against women are justified. The belief that women are inferior human beings in the eyes of God, gives excuses to the brutal husband who beats his wife, to the soldier who rapes a woman, the employer who has a lower pay scale for women employees, or parents who decide to abort a female embryo."[62]

Jimmy Carter, it must be stressed, is a man of faith and was one of the most religious people ever to get elected as President of the United States. He is a member of the Elders, a small group of retired leaders brought together by Nelson

Mandela, a group that also includes Archbishop Desmond Tutu. Therefore, they are not irreligious or anti-religious at all. They are calling on all religious leaders to "change all discriminatory practices within their own religions and traditions." Nicholas D. Kristof continued writing in his exceptionally relevant and insightful article that,

> There is of course plenty of fodder, in both the Koran and the Bible, for those who seek a theology of discrimination. The New Testament quotes St. Paul (1 Timothy 2) as saying that women "must be silent." Deuteronomy declares that if a woman does not bleed on her wedding night, "the men of her town shall stone her to death." An Orthodox Jewish prayer thanks God, "who has not made me a woman." The Koran stipulates that a woman shall inherit less than a man, and that a woman's testimony counts for half a man's.[63]

Lest we forget, religion is an intrinsic part of all cultures, not just in Arab nations. However, religion and culture are so intertwined in the Arab Middle East that most people in the world are unaware of, and would be amazed at, the level of interdependency. Author Reza Aslan writes tellingly on this subject saying: "*No religion exists in a vacuum. On the contrary, every faith is rooted in the soil in which it is planted. It is a fallacy to believe that people of faith derive their values primarily from their Scriptures. The opposite is true. People of faith insert their values into their Scriptures, reading them through the lens of their own culture, ethnic, nationalistic and even political perspectives.*"[64]

In my opinion, the toxic combination of culture and religion, the feeding frenzy they provide, and the lack of sophistication among most readers of Scripture are to blame for this cultural catastrophe regarding the status of women, religion in the public square, diversity, science, education, and social conditions generally.

Remember, we are not talking here about the cultural issues with which the West is struggling, such as irreligiousity, same-sex marriage, radical feminism, euthanasia, evolution teaching as a scientific fact, homosexuality, or other manifestations of perceived Western “decadence.” We are talking about basic human rights, elementary civil respect for human beings, such as the right to go to school, work, speak freely, and belong to whatever faith you desire.

Why do nations fail, and why is the Arab world failing miserably? The exclusion of women in most, if not all, Arab states, from public life, and from basic social, economic, and political participation in civic institutions is a major reason. Generation after generation, the illiteracy and marginalization of fifty percent of the Arab population has led to sterile, suffocating, and silent servitude and slavery at home, at work, and in the public square.

When half the women in Egypt still can’t read and write, how are their children going to join modernity, build a functioning democracy, have respect for other ethnic groups, talk about the need for the separation of mosque and state, or challenge religious dogma or the patriarchal system and outdated social norms and sexism? The same applies in varying degrees to Syria, Iraq, Saudi Arabia, Yemen, Libya, Jordan, and other Arab states that are mostly failing and living outside the march of history. Again, it’s the culture, stupid!

Chapter 6.

Sexual Repression as a Weapon of Mass Destruction

I cannot believe that a culture in which half of humanity is essentially in slavery to the other half, and in which all sexuality is treated as potentially damning, is a culture at peace with itself or the world.

—Andrew Sullivan

No doubt, sexual repression and segregation of men and women in some Islamic cultures has far-ranging cultural and psychological impacts. . . .

After all, it's hard to see why sexual frustration would be especially powerful during periods of "upheaval and disruption." Lewis, rather, attributes this rage and hatred to the challenge that the West poses to Islam as an alternative source of values and social organization, to the (correct) identification of the West as the source of "cataclysmic change" that threatens traditional ways, and to the humiliation of a

> *proud civilization bested economically, scientifically, and militarily by the West.*
>
> —CITIZEN CAIN, "Debunking the Sexual Repression Theory of Terrorism"

On June 25, 2015, the *Annahar* newspaper of Beirut, Lebanon—one of the leading publications in the Arab world—published a news report on how ISIS transported forty-two female hostages from Yazidi sect in the eastern part of Syria to the marketplace, where they were "sold" for between US$500 to $2000 per woman. The sellers told the ISIS fighters that the Yazidi women had converted to Islam, so it was permissible to marry them. The ISIS soldiers paid the agreed upon price out of their own pockets!

Worse still, on August 13, 2015, *The New York Times* published the following report on the sex slavery trade under the heading: "ISIS Enshrines a Theology of Rape." Here is the beginning of this surreal report:

> QADIYA, Iraq — In the moments before he raped the 12-year-old girl, the Islamic State fighter took the time to explain that what he was about to do was not a sin. Because the preteen girl practiced a religion other than Islam, the Quran not only gave him the right to rape her — it condoned and encouraged it, he insisted.
>
> He bound her hands and gagged her. Then he knelt beside the bed and prostrated himself in prayer before getting on top of her.

> When it was over, he knelt to pray again, bookending the rape with acts of religious devotion.
>
> "I kept telling him it hurts – please stop," said the girl, whose body is so small an adult could circle her waist with two hands. "He told me that according to Islam he is allowed to rape an unbeliever. He said that by raping me, he is drawing closer to God," she said in an interview alongside her family in a refugee camp here, to which she escaped after 11 months of captivity.
>
> The systematic rape of women and girls from the Yazidi religious minority has become deeply enmeshed in the organization and the radical theology of the Islamic State in the year since the group announced it was reviving slavery as an institution. Interviews with 21 women and girls who recently escaped the Islamic State, as well as an examination of the group's official communications, illuminate how the practice has been enshrined in the group's core tenets.[65]

Who are these people? Who are we? Is this fiction or reality? Can you separate these two solitudes from the Arab state of affairs? Are we back to the darkest periods of the Middle Ages? Is sexual repression a weapon of mass destruction?

The question that comes to mind is, did these thuggish fighters for this barbaric gang go to war in order to get a wife, to have sex and to hold a woman's hand? Have they done that before? Had they ever talked to or held a woman's hand before going to Syria, Iraq, Yemen, and Libya? Was sex on their minds? Was war a way to reach the unreachable in real life? Theories abound regarding the question of sexual repression and war, including terrorism. "Sex is a taboo in conservative Islamic countries. Young, unmarried couples are forced to seek out secret erotic oases. Books and play that are devoted to the all too human topic of sex incur the wrath of conservative religious officials and are promptly banned."[66]

However, using theology to advance the cause of sexual exploitation and rape is "innovative" thinking in its worst possible fashion. This mixture of selective usage of theological texts to abuse women is a modern-day plague. Sexual deprivation, alienation, loneliness, and utter aimlessness are creating monsters that the world has no choice but to deal with in every possible way.

Sexual Starvation

> *The problem with our societies is that the women are in love with their sons instead of their husbands, and the men are in love with their mothers instead of with their wives," she adds. "Men and women don't understand one another due to the fact that their dealings are not at all clear, as they don't spend enough time together or don't engage with each other enough.*
>
> *—Nadia Lamlili*

Arab culture is full of taboos. Sex is considered the mother of all taboos. Even a hint of it can, in conservative corners, make you a pariah within your own community. Public piety, however defined, is a virtue. It is a vice to speak of one's intimate feelings, to air one's inner thoughts and passions about nature's gifts to human beings, the gift of sexuality and romance.

Nature, in most Arab countries, is at the mercy of tradition, religious discourse, and dogmatic social norms. It is not accorded any supremacy, respect, or meaningful place in culture. Biology may be a science, but science takes second or third place to what the tribe or the cultural imperatives dictate. Biology is bottled up, imprisoned, tortured, and silenced like political dissident. Biological freedom is a crime. The totalitarian regimes have built a massive and elaborate system of jails all over the Arab world. Culture has done the same: It has built invisible Soviet-style concentration camps of the mind, imprisoning the young, the old, and the disoriented. Moreover, organized religion, which is an integral part of culture, has helped build this invisible prison by providing the legitimacy, the infrastructure, and the lifeblood of indispensible support over generations.

You may recall the fifteen girls who died in Mecca, Saudi Arabia, in 2002 due to a school fire after the "morality police" prevented them from escaping the burning building—and kept the firefighters from rescuing the schoolgirls—because they were not wearing headscarves and cloaks required in public places. In fact, they were "murdered" for all intents and purposes, burned because of who they were: girls imprisoned in a cultural cage, in a mental school of thought that considers costume, public show of piety and religious adherence to traditional concepts of what is permissible, more important and valuable than human life. If that is not an obsession with sexuality and the human anatomy, I don't know what is.

Commenting on Mona Eltahawy's essay "Why do they hate us?", Joumana Haddad, a Lebanese author and journalist said: "I agree with most of what she said but I think that the one thing that she might be reluctant to admit is that it's not about men hating women, it's about monotheistic religions hating women. They continually reinforce patriarchal standards and patterns that have existed long before. There is no harmony possible between monotheism and women's rights. The teachings deny women their dignity and rights."[67] Public piety and private practice are always at war in Arabic lands. This has been the pattern throughout human civilization. "Man has never reconciled himself to the Ten Commandments. We have seen Voltaire's view of history as mainly 'a collection of the crimes, follies and misfortunes' of mankind, and Gibbon's echo of that summary."[68]

All in all, when history, culture, and religion conspire together against women, then the odds are well understood. Attempts at reform, change, and the end of sexism are all worthy ideas meant to challenge the minds and passions of a particular generation at a particular time. Islam, Christianity, Judaism, and other religions all gave and continue to give women a slap on the face, imposing the loneliness of suffering upon which patriarchal societies have been based since the dawn of time. The heavy burden of history and tradition is overwhelming and hard to confront. Consider the following from Pope Francis, who is considered by many to be a modernizer. "Francis hasn't sanctioned any discussion of putting them there. When pressed about that by an Italian reporter last year, he reminded her that 'women were taken from a rib'. Was he ribbing her? He laughed and said so. But the metaphor remains, and it casts women as offshoots, even afterthoughts."[69]

An afterthought, an addendum to a masterpiece written by men, for men, and to men! How can sexism and obsession with women's bodies be eliminated when it is ingrained in the structure of organized religion all over the world? The issue of ordination of women as priests is one example of the monopoly of male power at the helm of the church.

> But the church's refusal to follow some other Christian denominations and ordain women undermines any progress toward equality that it trumpets or tries. Sexism is embedded in its structure, its flow chart. Men but not women get to preside at Mass. Men but never women wear the cassock of a cardinal, the vestments of a pope. Male clergy are typically called "father," which connotes authority. Women

> in religious orders are usually called "sister," which doesn't.[70]

We all know that sexuality and sexual desires are central characteristics to our species. Denying sexual pleasure has consequences on the individual, on society, and on culture. As author John Gray says, "We're all aware that sex tends to be more important to men while romance is more important to women, but we generally don't understand why."[71] In the Arab world, men are culturally caged when it comes to sex, and women and culturally shamed if they talk about, explore, or wonder about sexuality and its widespread taboos.

Is this creating a vacuum, a black hole, a weapon of mass destruction in Arab cultural landscape? The daily news reports from that corner of the world make one wonder every time one reads about or views a beheading by angry young men, a mass ethnic cleansing, a woman being sold in the market in ISIS territory, a stoning of a woman accused of adultery, or the killing of girls on their way to school. Sexual starvation may play a vital role in this regard, but it is certainly not the whole story. It is only a piece of the puzzle.

Perhaps the Arab world of more than 400 million inhabitants needs its own Magna Carta. That document, written in 1215, proved to be the seed that grew into contemporary conventions and set the stage for women's rights and the eventual emancipation in Western civilization. "Consider Article 8, for example: 'No widow shall be forced to marry so long as she wishes to live without a husband.'"[72] In that age, in that cultural milieu, that was a revolutionary piece of work and courageous thinking.

The Arab Middle East is still waiting for its Magna Carta!

Chapter 7.

Economic Echo: The Curse of Oil

Never before in history has a group of such relatively weak nations been able to impose with so little protest such a dramatic change in the way of life of the overwhelming majority of the rest of mankind. The poetic justice, if such it is, is that this "achievement" threatens their own stability, a perception that may be gradually dawning. Few political structures can sustain the accelerated rate of growth made possible by such an enormous transfer of wealth. Dislocations are bound to occur, which even more established political systems and traditions would find it difficult to handle. The institutions in most oil countries are not in that category.

—Henry Kissinger

The Arab world has the highest level of unemployment in the world, and youth unemployment rates are astronomical—averaging over 23 percent in the region. Worse, 60 percent of the Arab world is under the age of 30. In Tunisia, Egypt, Yemen, and potentially Jordan and Syria, the iron fist of repressive regimes were only able to postpone an inevitable political earthquake.

—www.counterpunch.org

The culture of dependency on oil in most of the Arab world has poisoned the minds of the old, the young, and the in-between. Natural resources can also be natural disasters. They create a cultural decay that destroys innovative thinking, instincts for inventions, and the entrepreneurial mindset while also spoiling younger generations and, above all, creating a culture of laziness and arrogance. We all know that easy money, easy life, and easy everything equal a difficult landing after reality comes knocking at the door. The Arab Spring was the first knock that shook the Arab body politic in every corner of its geography. The tremors are still being felt and will be felt for a long time, as history knows no rest, no final destination, and no compromise with artificial states with artificial economies.

When a culture has limited human capital, it has no capital at all. The opposite is also true. Look at Taiwan, for instance. No natural resources, all human capital. Look at Saudi Arabia—all natural resources, no human capital. Which country is going to survive, thrive, and advance? As writer Thomas Friedman says, "I always tell my friends in Taiwan: 'You're the luckiest people in the world. How did you get so lucky?' You have no oil, no iron ore, no forests, no diamonds, no gold, just a few small deposits of coal and natural gas—and because of that you developed the habits and culture of honing your people's skills, which turns out to be the most valuable and only truly renewable resource in the world today."[73]

Oil is indeed a curse. It provides a flood of money, financial security, comfort, luxury, high-rise buildings with endless amenities, shopping centres of the highest order, and so forth, but it provides nothing else. It provides no skills in science, math, innovation, or technological discoveries. All it does is grant nations the ability to import and purchase the latest Western gadgets, armaments, and toys for the elites and provide subsidies for the poor to keep them quiet. Saudi Arabia is a striking example of this. "The country ranks 73rd in the quality of its math and science education, according to the World Economic Forum—abysmally low for a rich country. Iran, despite 36 years of sanctions and a much lower per capita GDP, fares far better at 44."[74] Besides, all the production, work, industry, and performance in the marketplace in Saudi Arabia and most other oil-producing Arab countries, is performed by outsiders.

> One of every three people in Saudi Arabia is a foreigner. Two out of every three people with a job of any sort are foreign. And in Saudi Arabia's anemic private sector, fully nine out of ten people holding jobs are non-Saudi. . . . Saudi Arabia, in short, is a society in which all too many men do not want to work at jobs for which they are qualified: in which women by and large aren't allowed to work; and in which, as a result, most of the work is done by foreigners.[75]

On a broader scale, the following financial information from *Al Arabiya* newspaper provides a telling picture of what oil and its revenues in twenty-two Arab countries are all about.

Poking at the Beast: How much is the Arab world worth?

Arab oil-dependent countries resemble
a big whale that can't swim.

By EMAN EL-SHENAWI
Al Arabiya

Behind the numbers and economic jargon used to understand Middle East economies, a giant money beast lives and breathes. In some countries, the beast surges with strength to power through financial turbulence. But in other quieter Arab economies, they tell a more sluggish and less beast-like financial story.

With a mix of poverty and affluence, the Middle East is peppered with economic complexities; one might question how much the beast is actually worth?

The "Arab World" includes 22 countries in the Middle East and North Africa that form the Arab League and have a population of over 350 million, according to United Nations estimates.

As a breakdown of their value, the World Bank classifies Arab countries into income brackets. These brackets are low, lower middle, upper middle and high-income countries.

In the classification, the high-income Arab countries are Bahrain, Kuwait, Qatar, Saudi Arabia, and the United Arab Emirates. They are wealthy oil exporters that individually export up to 8.5 million barrels per day, which is the case for Saudi's current oil exports.

The Arab World's foreign assets are expected rise to a burgeoning $2.2 trillion this year, according to the Institute of International Finance (IIF), with the Gulf amassing $1.7 trillion of that amount. The figure reflects the substantial indebtedness of the region as it measures the value of the assets owned abroad, minus the value of the domestic assets owned by foreigners.

The biggest economies in the region are Saudi Arabia and Egypt respectively, measured by Gross Domestic Product (GDP) in real terms.

GDP is a measure of total national economic activity. It sets out the market value of all goods and services produced within a country in a given period. It is most commonly considered an indicator of a country's standard of living.

The largest economy, Saudi Arabia, with an estimated population of 25 million, has an annual GDP of $622 billion. Meanwhile Egypt, with a population of about 82 million, has an annual GDP of $500 billion. But neither Saudi nor Egypt has harnessed the highest growth rates in the region; a big economy does not mean highest growth. Qatar is the highest growing economy with a GDP per capita of $145,300.

GDP per capita (per person) is the total GDP divided by the resident population. It is widely used as an indicator to measure economic growth.

However, the total worth of Arab economies at $2.8 trillion does not mean much when compared to countries in the rest of the world. Germany for example, with a much smaller population than the Arab world (81 million), has a GDP of $2.9 trillion.[76]

On Oil, Wealth, and Corruption

Every nation wants to strike oil, and after it happens, nearly every nation is worse off for it. It may seem paradoxical, but finding a hole in the ground that spouts money can be one of the worst things that can happen to a country.

—Tina Rosenberg

Give me five years of $25-a-barrel oil and you'll see reformers strengthened in Iran and Saudi Arabia; they'll both have to tap their people instead of oil.

—Thomas L. Friedman

The proverbial resource curse is real. Over time, oil-dependent countries become an empty shell economically. Spouting money from the ground does not create jobs, establish a manufacturing sector, or enhance productivity. It is a proven fact that what economists call the "Dutch disease" is a curse that obliterates jobs in oil-dependent nations. This disease occurs when a country becomes so dependent on exporting natural resources that its currency rises in value, and then its manufacturing sector gets weakened as cheap imports become widespread and exports too expensive.

Furthermore, corruption becomes the norm rather than the exception. Political, economic, and social elites are all at the mercy of the ruling class and become servants to them. Exchange of favors becomes the way to do business. Concentration of wealth, bribery, corrupt politicians, and stale bureaucracy all coalesce to create a sorry state of affairs. Add to this the fact that petro-dependent countries, flush with money, go to war more often than other counties. Economists Paul Collier and Anke Hoeffler did some studies to confirm that. "They showed that if a third or more of a country's G.D.P. came from the exports of primary commodities, the likelihood of conflict was 22 percent. Similar countries that did not export commodities had a 1 percent chance."[77]

Single-crop economies are the worst when it comes to accountability, transparency, and tax collection. The profits from oil render tax collection unnecessary, thus creating a gulf between the people and their government, because they don't know how their money is being spent. Look at Nigeria, Chad, Venezuela, Angola, Saudi Arabia, Libya, and other petro economies in this regard.

The common definition of a "*rentier* state" is a state that is living on income from natural resources, such as oil, rather than collecting taxes.

> Where a government relies on financing from the tax base represented by its citizens, it is subject to questioning about how it allocates state resources. In a *rentier* mode of production, however, the government can act as a generous provider that demands no taxes or duties in return. This hand that gives can also take away, and the government is therefore entitled to require loyalty from its citizens invoking the mentality of the clan.[78]

In short, the state demands servitude, obedience, and silence. This creates, in return, a society of sheep-like citizens.

When there is money, there is stability, albeit artificial. When there is poverty, watch out for revolts and subjugation.

Efforts to diversify the economies of oil-dependent countries have been a mirage for a long time. Take Saudi Arabia. Diversification talk began in the 1900s, but when oil prices went up, that talk went down. Radical restructuring is needed to diversify, and an ultra-conservative kingdom like Saudi Arabia is not ready for it. Women in the workplace, employment for the youth, modernization of education, economic innovation, and scientific research for development are all absent. "Because change would include the slashing of some subsidies and a transformation of the country's stand against the rights of women, it would raise political tensions that the regime does not want to face. But avoiding restructuring and running out of money could end up being just as disruptive."[79]

Moreover, petro-dependent economies start treating education, innovation, creativity and entrepreneurialism as an afterthought. Look at the Arab world. Can you remember the last time you heard or read about a scientific or technical innovation that came from any of the twenty-two Arab League countries? What about other oil-dependent economies in the region? That's right, the number is zero.

The oil-rich countries of the Arab world may be expanding and teaching more of their young generations. However, as Lebanese Minister of Education Elias Bou Saab told me in May, 2015, at the Lebanese Diaspora Energy Conference held in Beirut when I asked him why Lebanon and other Arab counties are not improving or changing, as we witnessed the upheaval in the burning region, "There is a huge difference between learning and being educated. We are teaching our young but they are not getting educated properly." Education means critical thinking not repetition or memorization of data. Education means growth, to change as the facts and evidence compel you to see the world anew. Education means to question authority, rebel against injustice, and never be silent in the presence of sectarian, stupid, or superstitious talk or debate. Education means to respect your heritage and traditions but never to be held hostage by them or be shackled to them for eternity. Education means to think anew in order to act anew, to strive for a better tomorrow, not to live in the past as a glorious endeavour, and to know that if you don't have natural resources, you use your educational tools to become resourceful.

Furthermore, "Education," says author Charles Varle, "is a companion which no misfortune can depress, no crime destroy, no enemy alienate, no despotism enslave. At home, a friend; abroad, an introduction; in solitude, a solace; and in society, an ornament. Without it, what is man? A splendid slave, a reasoning savage." .A truly educated society is a passport to civility, prosperity and real living. Learning is not enough: we must be educated.

When summarizing the difference between education and learning, the following six points are essential:

1. Education is the process of imparting knowledge, values, skills and attitudes which can be beneficial to an individual. On the contrary, learning is the process of adopting knowledge, values and skills.

2. Learning is the basic instinct possessed by all individuals. On the other hand, education is acquired by individuals.

3. Learning is said to be an ongoing process. Education is something that one gets at some point in their life.

4. Learning is an informal process, and education is a formal process.

5. Learning is knowledge gained through experience, and education is knowledge gained through teaching.

6. Education is something that an individual gets from an outside source. On the other hand, learning is something that evolves in the inner self.[80]

Therefore, oil-dependent countries in the Arab world are sinking deep into a quagmire of money that is a cancer on the body politic. This manufactured prosperity is not only fictional; it makes societal progress unlikely. The governing elites are awash in money with no incentive to do anything but preserve and accumulate more of the same. The populace is being bought with their own money, bribed handsomely to stay silent and obedient. The young are frozen in time, unwilling or unable to make the changes necessary. Unemployment will continue to rise, because oil money does not create jobs outside its own circle. And the Arab world will continue to go in circles, spinning its wheels, going nowhere fast!

Note: The falling oil prices in 2015–2016 are of little significance to the task at hand. The Arab states that depend on oil exports are not going to change any time soon. It will be business-as-usual for the next few decades. Then watch out when new technologies and innovations in the energy sector play havoc in these societies. It will not be a pretty scene to watch.

The following provide a summary of the current state of the Arab world.

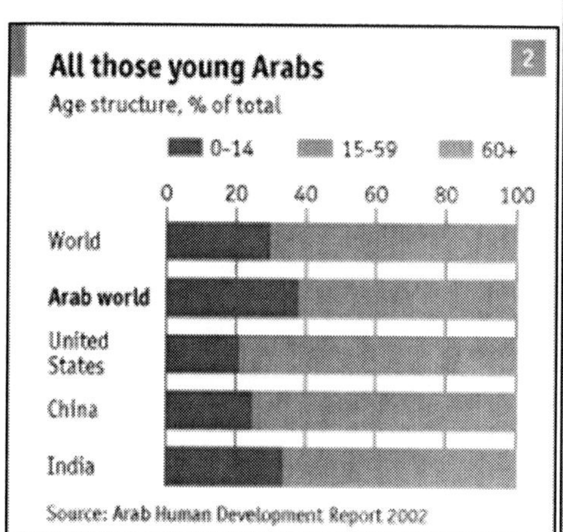
All those young Arabs
2
Age structure, % of total
0-14
15-59
60+
0
20
40
60
80
100
World
Arab world
United States
China
India
Source: Arab Human Development Report 2002

Ever further behind
1
Average rankings
HDI
AHDI (see text)
0
20
40
60
80
100
North America
Europe
Australasia
Latin America & the Caribbean
South & East Asia
Arab countries
Source: Arab Human Development Report 2002

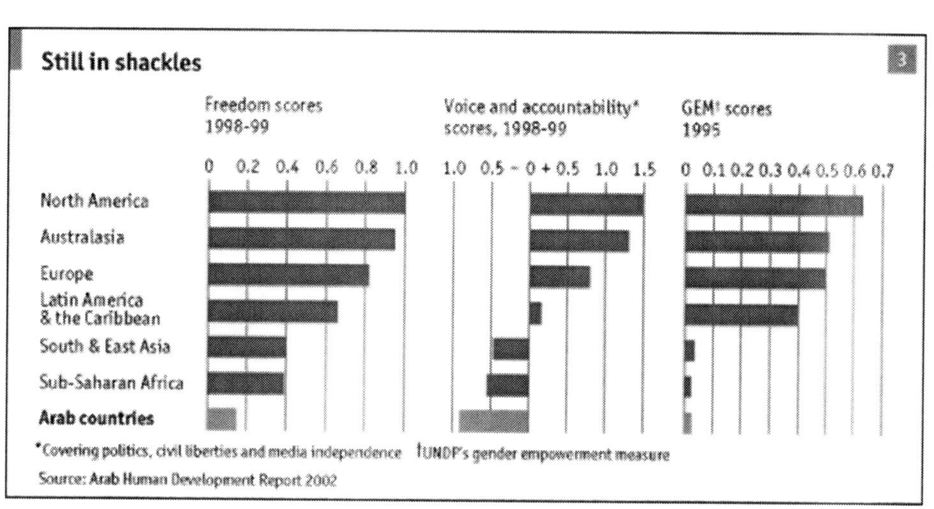
Still in shackles
3
Freedom scores 1998-99
Voice and accountability* scores, 1998-99
GEM† scores 1995
0 0.2 0.4 0.6 0.8 1.0
1.0 0.5 − 0 + 0.5 1.0 1.5
0 0.1 0.2 0.3 0.4 0.5 0.6 0.7
North America
Australasia
Europe
Latin America & the Caribbean
South & East Asia
Sub-Saharan Africa
Arab countries
*Covering politics, civil liberties and media independence
†UNDP's gender empowerment measure
Source: Arab Human Development Report 2002

Chapter 8.

Rhetoric as Romance

The proneness to exaggeration he describes was amply displayed in the Gulf war by the exhortations of Saddam Hussein to the Arabs in the "mother of all battles." This penchant for rhetoric and use of hyperbole were a feature of the Arab press during the war....It is also an apt example of the Arab tendency to substitute words for action and a desired outcome for a less palatable reality, or to indulge in wishful thinking.

—Norvell B. De Atkine

You can't eat sharia. . . . The uprising was not about changing people, but changing our mindset.

—Mohamed Elbaradei, Egyptian scientist/activist

The Arab culture adores rhetoric and speechmaking. It is in love with the Arabic language for its own sake, not as an instrument to be used to communicate and function socially but as an end by itself. The Arabic language is an aphrodisiac and a substitute for the harsh reality on the ground. Poetry is a form of social medicine. Composition is viewed as a literary and social achievement.

Truth be told, the Arabic language is majestic. It is one of the most beautiful, elegant, and substantive languages on Earth. I love it! But like science, religion, medicine, or any other social phenomenon, it has been used and abused throughout history by tyrants, the clergy, politicians, and merchants.

On Classic Arabic, Rhetoric, and Faith

The trouble with the Arabic language is that it is mesmerizing and intoxicating and powerful when delivered by professional speakers and rhetoricians. The richness it contains is limitless and deliciously seductive. It is considered, moreover, from a cultural and religious perspective, as exceptional and divine. "Native speakers of Arabic have long claimed that Arabic is far more than a language: rather, the language of Islam, the language chosen by God to speak to mankind, influences how a person perceives the world and expresses reality. . . . Abdelkader Yefsah, a sociologist, recently wrote that the use of Arabic language 'leads straight to . . . the primacy of the religious over all other activity.'"[81] The connection, therefore, that Arab culture draws between its language and religion, in this case, Islam, gives religious, political, and social elites more reasons to utilize the power of the Arabic language and its inherent magic to bolster their claims and advance their legitimacy. "Even the most secular Arab nationalists (such as the Ba'thist variants in Syria and Iraq) must appeal to Islamic symbolism to bolster sagging legitimacy and to mobilize the masses (as Saddam Husayn Hussein did in his wars against Iran and the U.S.-led coalition). Hence, Arab nationalism has, however inadvertently, contributed to the rise of Islamism."[82]

The flowery language, the bombastic rhetoric, the religious messianic mixture of language and faith, the sublime poetry and passionate words that breathe fire, the echo of battles won and lost through phrases and sentences that are full of fury and sound signifying nothing, are too common, too alive, and too tiresome to notice these days given the state of affairs in Arab lands. Leaders give speeches for two to three hours. Sermons from religious lecterns run non-stop for hours. Speeches at conferences, political events, and special occasions are notorious for their length, as if by virtue of making a speech or uttering a sentence or saying many words repetitively the mission is accomplished, the task completed, the battle won. Words, fiery words, are considered enough to replace reality or to camouflage it.

Poetry and poets were revered and respected like saints in Arab culture and history. They were accorded special privileges and access to the most powerful and influential leaders. Why? Poetry and poems are great entertainment and an artful cultural heritage. Poets are merchants of words and sentences, and they beautify the language. But they are not producers or manufacturers or inventors of any product or service that can be deemed socially or scientifically beneficial to society. Yet that was, and is, the norm, in Arab culture—to adore poetry and poets, speakers and rhetoric for their own sake without questioning the cost-benefit ratio. What is it for beside entertainment and diversion? What is it contributing to the well being of society? Is it useful to continue down this road forever? "The unexamined life is not worth living," Socrates said. Nietzsche was also correct when he said: "I have left the house of the scholars, and I have slammed the door behind me. Too long I sat hungry at their table."[83]

Using rhetoric to romance and massage the masses with empty phrases and exciting words has been the practice throughout history and in all civilizations. This is a given. What is not a given, however, is the impulse in the Arab culture to employ the bombastic nature and powerful appeal of language in all stages of life: war and peace, life and death, prosperity and poverty. Seldom does one look back to see if the rhetoric matched reality or the desired results.

Gibran Kahlil Gibran (1883–1931) is Lebanon's best-known poet, philosopher, and author. He wrote his masterpiece *The Prophet,* and included a section on "Talking," saying:

> You talk when you cease to be at peace with your thoughts;
>
> And when you can no longer dwell in the solitude of your heart you live in your lips, and sound is a diversion and a pastime.
>
> And in much of your talking, thinking is half murdered.
>
> For thought is a bird of space, that in a cage of words may indeed unfold its wings but cannot fly.
>
> ...And there are those who talk, and without knowledge or forethought reveal a truth which they themselves do not understand.
>
> And there are those who have the truth within them, but they tell it not in words.[84]

Gibran was a pariah in his own culture. The political, religious, and sectarian establishments did not welcome him. Organized religious groups tried to ban his books, especially *The Prophet,* in Lebanon and in the Arab Middle East. He was the ultimate Renaissance man and author in a world that is still living in the Middle Ages. His name and his quotes are everywhere—except where it matters most: in the minds, deeds, passions, practices, and habits of everyday Arab people. No traces of Gibran's thinking or messages are evident in the Lebanese or Arab culture.

Summary

Language is our window to the world. It is a vital part of our identity, our culture. The Arabic language reflects the Arabic mind. It is an axiom that every time a person speaks, his or her mind is on parade. Confronted with stagnation, decline, economic meltdown, sectarian divisions, totalitarian regimes, corruption, nepotism, religious domination, unemployment, brain drain, lack of freedom, an out-dated educational system, oppression and marginalization of women, a weak middle class, no separation of state and mosque, no social contract, and above all, no real concept of citizenship, the Arab citizen turns to language manipulation to compensate.

The tyrant, the merchants, the elites, and the media all do the same. Language becomes a refuge, a medicine, an escape, a ploy to defy reality, the world, and even death. Excessive employment of language becomes a second chance at survival and life. In Lebanese culture, for instance, there is a kind of poetry called "*zajal*". It is a popular style of sophistry of words and sentences that is improvised by professional poets for popular entertainment. Like political speeches, poetry is used to inflame unrealistic, unattainable, and illusionary flight from what is doable, practical, and possible in real life. In this sense, it is another form of religious discourse designed to create an alternative reality, given the unbearable and deadly reality that actually exists. It is an escape, but like all escapes, in the end it is counterproductive, because it leads people to rely on nothingness and fantasy.

Enough negativity. Enough inspection inside the black box of a culture in historical crisis trying hopelessly to find its way out. In the next chapter, I will shed the light on the bright side of Arab culture and its peoples.

Chapter 9.

The Golden Side of Arab Culture

> During all the first part of the Middle Ages, no other people made as important a contribution to human progress as did the Arabs, if we take this term to mean all those whose mother-tongue was Arabic, and not merely those living in the Arabian peninsula. For centuries, Arabic was the language of learning, culture and intellectual progress for the whole of the civilized world with the exception of the Far East. From the IXth to the XIIth century there were more philosophical, medical, historical, religiuos, astronomical and geographical works written in Arabic than in any other human tongue.
>
> —Phillip Hitti in 'Short History of the Arabs.'

"We are naked," wrote Samir Attallah in describing the Lebanese and Arab conditions in the *Annahar* newspaper on February 25, 2015. That was the undisputable state of Arab lands measured by the military, security, economic, religious, and social upheaval visiting the region. Internal, regional, and international elements and conditions all came together to create the perfect firestorm of historic proportions.

But it wasn't always like that. On the contrary, at one point, Arab culture was a shining city on a hill. This lasted for centuries. Here are some of Arab culture's most notable achievements, and this list is far from exhaustive.

> A THOUSAND years ago, the great cities of Baghdad, Damascus and Cairo took turns to race ahead of the Western world. Islam and innovation were twins. The various Arab caliphates were dynamic superpowers—beacons of learning, tolerance and trade. Yet today the Arabs are in a wretched state. Even as Asia, Latin America and Africa advance, the Middle East is held back by despotism and convulsed by war. . . . Education underpinned its primacy in medicine, mathematics, architecture and astronomy. Trade paid for its fabulous metropolises and their spices and silks. And, at its best, the Arab world was a cosmopolitan haven for Jews, Christians and Muslims of many sects, where tolerance fostered creativity and innovation.[85]

Moreover, following Mohammed, two dynasties dominated Arab culture and were the leading forces behind Arab supremacy and its outstanding civilization. These were the Umayyad caliphs, located in Damascus from 661 to 750, and the Abbasid caliphs, established in Baghdad from 751 to 1258.

> Arab rulers brought intellectual Jews, Christians, Greeks, Persians, and Indians to Baghdad and other centers of learning during the Abbasid dynasty. These foreign intellectuals contributed elements from their own cultures to the development of Arab culture. The works of

> Plato and Aristotle were translated from Greek into Arabic before they were translated into other European languages. Indian scientists brought the concept of "zero" to the Arabs, who combined it with Arabic numbers and transmitted the mathematical systems of algebra, geometry, and trigonometry to Europe.[86]

Scientists and scholars also know that during the Abbasid dynasty, Arab scientists discovered Euclid's theory that the eye emanates rays, chemists introduced the concept of alcohol, and medical scholars complied the world's first medical encyclopedia. (Source: Encyclopedia of World Cultures.)

> Arabic civilization from the eighth to the thirteenth centuries excelled in all fields of knowledge. The importance of Arabic culture in the history of world culture was based on the discovery of new means of scientific, religious, philosophical, and artistic cognition of man and the world.

> Hispano-Arabic civilization flourished brilliantly during the tenth through 15th centuries. Its centers were Cordoba, Seville, Malaga, and Granada. The greatest progress was made in astronomy, mathematics, chemistry, and medicine. The progressive line of Arab philosophy—al-Farabi (c. 870–950) and Avicenna (ibn Sina, 980–1037)—was continued, for example, in the works of Averroes (ibn Rushd, 1126–1198). Some of the greatest literary works of Arabic culture were created in poetry and literature. Monuments of Hispano-Moorish architecture and applied art achieved worldwide renown. A

> great achievement of Arabic culture in the late Middle Ages was the creation of a historical-philosophical theory of social development by the historian and sociologist Ibn-Khaldun (1332–1406).[87]

Furthermore, in the first part of the nineteenth century, the Arab world, after a long domination by the Ottoman Empire, which lasted more than five hundred years, experienced an economic and political renaissance, resulting in national liberation movements and political emancipation from the Turkish and colonial masters. It ended in the formation of the current independent Arab state system, which is being challenged again like never before.

Some Golden Features of Arab Culture

For the sake of fairness and objectivity, let us examine the bright side of Arab culture from historical and current perspectives. The following does not exhaust the potential list.

Family and Community

The family unit in Arab culture is considered a kingdom of happiness, achievement, and the ultimate human purpose. It is elevated to an almost scared status. Family life is above all else. It is the unit that functions even if society, the state, or the environment is in chaos. Loyalty to the family is often considered more important than loyalty to one's country, citizenship, society, tribe, or the world at large. Men have their roles, and women have theirs. Family is the final refuge in case darkness descends. In times of triumph or despair, it offers the Arab person a guarantee of survival. Throughout history, family has functioned as the only reliable social safety net.

Faith

Faith as a guiding light can be a form of pure piety. Understood from this perspective, piety is valued a great deal in Arab culture. Many view faith as exclusive and divisive. Few practice it as a call to duty, sharing, and charity. Faith can be an internal jihad to become a better person and a better citizen in a better community.

Honor and Respect

Reputation, honor, and social acceptance play a significant part in Arab culture. Saving face, being in good standing within your family, neighbourhood, tribe, and community are all essential characteristics of the Arab social landscape. Leaving a good impression on people is also essential. Never criticize people publicly. Doing so is a taboo. Being indirect and discreet is valued.

Taking Care of the Elderly

Reverence for elderly people, including both men and women, is a golden Arab social tradition. Families of different generations often live under the same roof. Sending fathers and mothers to old age institutions is a taboo and carries with it a social stigma. Very few people do that, unlike the Western world. It is believed that wisdom comes with age, so sage people are respected and revered. Tolerance of the older generation knows no limitation. It is expected and practiced. It has been the Arab tradition for centuries.

Hospitality

My memories of my grandfather Ellia Nasrallah in Lebanon, who was a well-known local leader of the village called Kfar Meshki in the Bekaa Valley, center on how he opened his house almost twenty-four hours a day to locals and strangers alike in order to invite them for coffee, dinner, or social conversation. Hospitality was in his blood. Helping a person in need or a hungry man was job number one. I remember an endless flow of visitors from every corner of the country and from all sects and religions. Giving is a traditional Arab trait. Helping the needy and the dispossessed is a duty.

Children as the Jewels of Life

In Arab culture, children are the beginning and the end of everything in life. They are considered God's gifts, grace, and the oxygen for survival. People sacrifice their lives for their children. They are ready to endure torture, hardship, agony, and endless misery to give them a better shot at life or a better future. Couples who don't have children for physical or financial reasons are viewed as incomplete or living an unfulfilling life.

Friendship and Loyalty

True friends are second brothers and sisters in Arab culture. In most cases, friendships last for life. Loyalty to one's family, tribe, and friends is non-negotiable. True friendship knows no boundaries in times of war or peace, abundance or poverty.

In addition to the above, food, music, dance, attachment to places (mourning the relics), poetry, and literature are all virtues of Arab culture. Arabic culture values stability and people become attached to places of residence, worship and family. They value tradition and familiarity. Food, for instance, is not only a necessary physical aspect of daily livies. It is for family cohesion and for friendship, and a meal could take hours to enjoy. Lebanese cuisine, for instance, is now competing with Italian food for international market share. Many musical instruments were invented in Arab lands during the Golden Age. The "debki" dance, for example, is a cherished cultural artistic jewel.]

Summary

Unfortunately, the challenges facing the Arab culture and the negative aspects discussed in previous chapters outweigh the positive features. Since the end of the thirteenth century and the defeat of the rationalist school of thought that propelled the Arab Golden Age, the Arab culture, peoples, states, and civilization have paid a heavy price in blood and treasure. It is time to bring back that rationalist tradition so we can rescue the Arab world from its present black hole. It is time to rejoin modernity, history, and life itself. It is time also to think anew in order to act anew. To capitalize on the cultural heritage of the golden days, and to rejoin the march of history and be great once more.

It is time to be happy again!

Chapter 10.

Global Perceptions of Arab Peoples and Arab Culture

I believe Western culture — rule of law, universal sufferage, etc. — is preferable to Arab culture: that's why there are millions of Muslims in Scandinavia, and four Scandinavians in Syria. Follow the traffic. I support immigration, but with assimilation.

—Mark Steyn, author

We are a thick skinned people with empty souls. We spend our days playing dice, chess, or sleeping — and we say we are the best people that ever came to mankind.

—Nizar Qabbani, Arab poet

The world has been asking itself this question for a long time: What is the matter with the Arab peoples, their culture, and direction given their rich history and contribution to human civilization in contrast to today's sad state of affairs? The perceptions for the past few decades have been a mixed bag of utter bewilderment and constant concern for the collapse of the Arab state system, cultural decay, and stalled development on most levels. In fact, as Austrian psychotherapist Alfred Alder says, what happens is important, but how it is perceived can have even more important consequences. We must remember this: pay attention to perception.

The daily news is a reminder of what is wrong with the Arab Middle East. Terrorism, human smuggling flooding the borders of Europe, and the refugee influx from Syria, Iraq, Yemen, Libya, and other parts of the globe. Suicide bombings in marketplaces, churches, and mosques, not to mention the barrel bombs dropping on civilians in many parts of war-ravaged Syria. Add to this the sectarian strife between the Sunni and Shia sects of Islam and the massacres in Tunisia and Egypt that target tourists. The terrible influx of bad news in never-ending, especially from the Arab corner of the globe. What is going on here?

Arab Culture in American and Western Minds

Classically, in the American mind, Arab culture was the culture of camels. Now it is associated with terrorism, tyranny, and tribulation. Sadly enough, although these views don't paint the complete picture, they are real, present, and enduring. Edward W. Said did not mince words when he wrote this assessment of how Americans perceive Arab culture and peoples:

> For decades in America there has been a cultural war against the Arabs and Islam: appalling racist caricatures of Arabs and Muslims suggest that they are all either terrorists or sheikhs, and that the region is a large arid slum, fit only for profit or war. The very notion that there

> might be a history, a culture, a society—indeed many societies—has not held the stage for more than a moment or two, not even during the chorus of voices proclaiming the virtues of "multiculturalism."[88]

In June 2006, the Pew Research Centre published a study on Global Attitudes and Trends called "The Great Divide: How Westerners and Muslims View Each Other." The following quote from the report highlights many relevant issues: "Many in the West see Muslims as fanatical, violent, and as lacking tolerance. Meanwhile, Muslims in the Middle East and Asia generally see Westerners as selfish, immoral and greedy—as well as violent and fanatical."[89]

The study also highlights the differences in perceptions regarding the controversial Muhammed cartoon incident that same year. "Most people in Jordan, Egypt, Indonesia and Turkey blame the controversy on Western nation's disrespect for the Islamic religion. In contrast, majorities of Americans and Western Europeans who have heard of the controversy say Muslims' intolerance to different points of views is more to blame."[90]

More fundamental differences emerge when perceptions about the role of women and men and attitudes about women in general are discussed. "The chasm between Muslims and the West is also seen in judgments about how the other civilization treats women. The Western public, by lopsided margins, do not think of Muslims as 'respectful of women.' But half or more in four of the five Muslim publics surveyed say the same thing about people in the West."[91]

Moreover, anti-Muslim sentiment in the United States seems to be on the rise, as confirmed by Public Policy Polling (PPP) conducted in North Carolina, a southern state, and published in *The New York Times* on September 29, 2015. Consider these results:

Do you think a Muslim should ever be allowed to be President of the United States, or not?

- A Muslim should be allowed to be President of the United States: 16 percent

- A Muslim should not be allowed to be President of the United States: 72 percent

- Not sure: 12 percent"

Do you think the religion of Islam should be legal or illegal in the United States?

- Islam should be legal in the United States: 40 percent

- Islam should be illegal in the United States: 40 percent

- Not sure: 20 percent"

The following chart is also instructive to the subject at issue:[92]

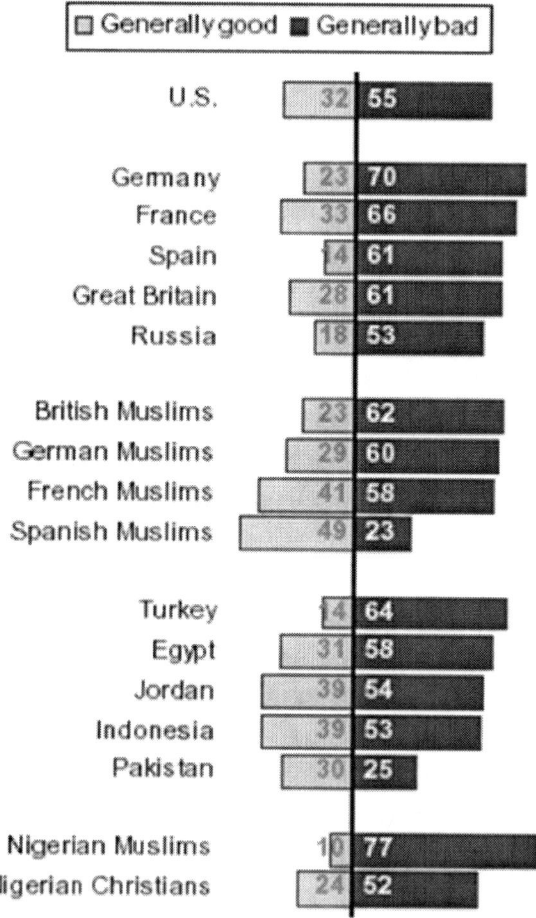

(Further note: After the California mass shooting on December 02, 2015, and the killing of 14 innocent people, which was a planned terrorist attack, the backlash against Muslims in the United States intensified and the political attacks became daily occurance especially by Republican presidential candidates the likes of Donald Trump.)

Canada mirrors the United States for the most part in regard to its perception of Arab culture, albeit in a more benign, civil, and subtle way. Traditionally, Canada has had an even-handed approach to the Palestinian-Israeli conflict, tilting a little to the Israeli side. But under the conservative regime of Stephen Harper, Canada's foreign policy undertook a dramatic and decidedly undiplomatic approach to the Arab-Israeli problem by aligning itself completely with Israel on all issues.

Although the Arab diaspora in Canada is about 400,000 strong, their political and social influence is weak and dispersed because of political and religious divisions and lack of co-ordination between various segments of this sizable community, hence its lack of respect, influence, and lobbying power.

Generally speaking, Canadians, like Americans, get their perception of Arab culture from Hollywood movies, the daily news, terrorist acts, women's issues like the hijab and honor killings, refugee crises, and the media. The constant bombardment of reports of conflict and fighting in the Arab Middle East does not help in changing the negative perception of the Arab state of affairs, which has been ingrained in the minds and hearts of Canadians for decades. In fact, during the 2015 federal election campaign, the niqab became a hot issue after a court ruled that a woman should be allowed to cover her face while attending a citizenship ceremony. The Conservative government at that time appealed the decision to the Supreme Court of Canada.

Writing in *The Globe and Mail*, journalist and writer Margaret Wente offered this insightful commentary on the Canadian attitudes regarding the niqab.

> But if there is one issue that strikes a nerve with Canadians, that is it. Public opposition to the niqab is deep and wide. A recently released Leger poll, commissioned by the government and conducted in March (2015), found that more than four out of five people—82 per

> cent—supported the Conservatives' position that there is no place for niqab in citizenship court. In Quebec, the figure was 93 per cent. . . . It is really a debate about our values, and equality, and the limits of tolerance.[93]

Although the niqab is not confined to the Arab Middle East—other cultures, such as Pakistan and Afghanistan, also use it—the attention almost always comes upon the Arabs as they are in the news daily given what is going on in that part of the globe.

In Europe, the Arab Middle East is closer geographically and more relevant historically. The crisis of the refugees from Syria, Iraq, Libya, and other African countries flooding European shores in 2015 concentrated the minds of the European populations and brought the crisis home. In fact, the photo of Alan Kurdi, a little Syrian refugee boy who drowned and whose body was found lying on a Turkish beach in the summer of 2015, was the ultimate symbol of the extent of the Syrian human catastrophe.

The Muslim population in Europe in considerable in terms of numbers. According to Pew Research Centre, "Germany and France have the largest Muslim population among European Union member countries. As of 2010, there were 4.8 million Muslims in Germany (5.8% of the country's population) and 4.7 million Muslims in France (7.5%). In Europe overall, however, Russia's population of 14 million Muslims (10%) is the largest on the continent."(http://www.pewresearch.org/fact-tank/2015/11/17/5-facts-about-the-muslim-population-in-europe/) Islamophobia has always been an issue in France, Germany, Italy, and Britain. In this regard, the onslaught of refugees is a double-edged sword: It has revealed the human side of many European nations, such as Germany, which has welcomed thousands of refugees, but it has also brought out the ugly side of discrimination and inhumane ways of dealing with such a tragedy, as is the case with Hungary.

The perception of Arabs and Arab culture remains negative for the most part in most European. The collapse of the Arab Spring, the disintegration of many states in the Arab Middle East, and the constant conflicts afflicting the area all leave a bad image of a civilization that has lost its core.

Arab Culture and the Rest of the World

For China, a rising superpower, the Arab world is not only far away, it is also irrelevant to China's domestic and foreign policy. China's economic development, however, depends on importing many vital natural resources, and chief among them is oil. From this perspective, the Arab Middle East is of vital strategic interest to China's leadership. The flow of oil is a matter of national security. Any other political, social, or economic aspect is of minor importance. Therefore, China's perception of Arab culture is limited to its economic needs and does not extend any further than that.

Russia, on the other hand, has had a longstanding problem with its Muslim.population, especially in Chechnya. During the Cold War, Russia played a significant role in Middle Eastern affairs and continues to do so now, especially in Syria. From the Soviet Union days to Vladimir Putin's regime, Russia's competition with the West in the Arab world has been legendary and continues to be so today, although in varying degrees. Russia is now involved with Turkey, after the Russian warplane was shot down by Turkey, in direct competition even enomosity. The image of Russia in the Arab world is being challenged especially in the Sunni dominated countries.

Russia's perception of Arab culture is also ambivalent and focuses of self-interest and national security without any consideration for humanitarian, cultural, or social factors. Sales of armaments and geopolitical balance of power politics are more important to the leaders of the Kremlin than the success of the Arab Spring, social development, or economic growth in the region. Vladimir Putin is on a crusade to reassert and reinvigorate Russia's standing in the world as a global power at any cost. Syria is just another stop along that road, as is Ukraine. Writing in *The Washington Post,* foreign policy expert Anne Applebaum states that, "Of course, the Syrian people aren't really the point here—and the Russian people aren't either. Putin's invasion of Ukraine has been bad for his countrymen and bad for his country—for its economy, its image, its influence—and a tragedy for Ukraine. Expect the same kind of outcome from his incursion into Syria too."[94] All in all, Russia cares more about politics than culture. The Arabs are a means to an end, not an end by themselves.

In summary, the perceptions and images of Arab culture and peoples are becoming intertwined with reality as it has unfolded since 2010. The axiom that "perception is reality" is sadly relevant in this regard. This has little to do with decent Arab citizens and lots to do with the broader cultural forces at work.

The fact remains that modern Arab culture is lacking on most fronts. It is lacking a core, a set of values, and relevance in a world of fast-moving change, an intensity of being alive, a direction, and a vision. It is adrift, swimming against the tide of history. The world is wondering about the future of over 400 million people, and their perceptions are not encouraging. Alas, endless miserable nights are ahead. No end is in sight for this cataclysmic cultural catastrophe.

Chapter 11.

Freedom Famine: The Deficit of Freedom in the Arab World

The Russian Communists have not solved, nor will their violent and repressive methods ever enable them to solve, the fundamental problem of human society, the problem of freedom. For in freedom only can human society flourish and bear fruit. Freedom alone gives meaning to life: without it life is unbearable.

—Benedetto Croce, October 1932

"Freedom to" is the freedom to live your life, speak your mind, start your own political party, build your own business, vote for any candidate, pursue happiness, and be yourself, whatever your sexual, religious or political orientation.

—Thomas L. Friedman

And if it is a despot you would dethrone, see first that his throne erected within you is destroyed. For how can a tyrant rule the free and the proud, but for a tyranny in their own freedom and a shame in their own pride.

—Khalil Gibran, *The Prophet*

Tyrannical and totalitarian regimes are deadly forms of human servitude. They destroy the spirit of life, the energy of the populace, leaving society as an empty shell. Once a tyrant is overthrown, nothing fills the vacuum except religious discourse, political upheaval, and tribal infighting. The individual in the Arab culture does not exist outside his or her community, tribe, or sect, hence the demise of the Arab Spring.

Again, I am using the Socratic style of being *a topos*, which means "out of place," and talking in disturbing and frank ways about my place, community, and society. This is the philosopher's method of using straight talk to deliver a message of what is going on among his people. I am, however, neither Socrates nor a person who remained in his birthplace pretending to be an outsider from within. I am outside. I am still *a topos*.

One of the most troubling aspects of the Arab world is its cultural misunderstanding of the word "freedom." In most Arab countries, the cultural perception of freedom is synonymous with the prevalence of promiscuity, decadence, teen pregnancy, rape, porn, divorce, child abuse, and the breakdown of the family unit. To many Arabs, it also means freedom to criticize and disobey religious values and religious authorities and instil new values in the younger generation that are at variance with established norms. This is considered a threat to the established order.

Freedom, however, as understood in the Western world or most advanced societies, is freedom to think independently, freedom of conscience, freedom of speech, of assembly, freedom of association, freedom of political thought, freedom to marry outside of your faith, freedom of the media, freedom *of* religion as well as freedom *from* religion. This chapter will deal with the concept of freedom in the Arab world and why it is such a cultural pariah crushed under the weight of history, tradition, conformity, religion, and tyranny.

Religion and Freedom in the Arab World

> *The al-Saudis responded by forging a new bargain with their religious conservatives: Let us stay in power and we'll give you a freer hand in setting social norms, relations between the sexes and religious education inside Saudi Arabia—and vast resources to spread the puritanical, anti-women, anti-Shiite, anti-pluralistic Sunni Wahhabi fundamentalism to mosques and schools around the world.*
>
> —Thomas L. Friedman

Since religion, as we discussed in chapter 4, is considered in the Arab-Islamic world as an integral whole encompassing all aspects of life from the cradle to the grave, any concept of personal or societal freedom must exist under that roof. All aspects of life, as Dr. Ahmad F. Yousif writes, become spiritualized and, indeed, acts of worship.

Therefore, for freedom, in the Western sense, to exist, it must conform to the Islamic narrative. However, this in itself is a contradiction of terms and an impossible task. In many Western countries, freedom *of* religion comes with freedom *from* religion. From this perspective, the concept of freedom in the Arab world is culturally and religiously bound and limited by nature and necessity to that background. It is not freedom, as we understand the word.

In February 2004, way before the advent of the Arab Spring, an intellectual debate was held in Beirut at the St. George Hospital University. It included the late revered writer and statesman Ghassan Tueni and famous poet and critic Adonis—official name Ali Ahmad Said Esper—who debated the sad state of affairs in the Arab world and called for a cultural revolution. Adonis offered a brilliant religious, social, and political critique of the Arab political culture focusing on the following themes.

First, the singularity of the religious discourse and its claims to the ultimate truth necessitates the following: that God has sent his last messenger, his last message, and his last word. Therefore, man has nothing to add to or subtract from that message. The truth is told, known, case closed. Man's task is only to believe, follow, and obey God's message. Furthermore, added Adonis, the word of God is complete, final, and man's interpretations or *ijtihad* is limited and defective, and the words of God become synonymous with reality if not reality itself. Human beings are just witnesses. The truth has been sent to us, and we exist to follow the system of thought and practices as dictated by the message. Thus, freedom is non-existent except in this regard.

Second, to Adonis, the religious narrative was copied and translated to the political realm. The unilateralism of religious discourse was carried to the body politic. They get intertwined and became twins in body, spirit, and practice, hence the "freedom famine" and the beginning of the catastrophic collapse of the Arab world.

Third, by capturing the essence of one of the intrinsic problems in Arab culture, Adonis and Tueni highlighted the role of authority in Arab societies. By hijacking the truth, the religious establishments put itself outside of history, beyond criticism, and beyond the reach of the laws of the land or its norms. It has positioned itself above all human institutions.

This view of the truth as the domain of authority has been the hallmark of Arab political culture for centuries. In modern times, it is still the essence of traditional Arab thinking. As Michael P. Lynch writes brilliantly, "*Consider the idea that the real essence of truth is Authority—that is, what is true is whatever God, or the King or the Party commands or accepts, that is a reductive definition, one that still lurks in the background of many people's worldview. It has also been used over the centuries to stifle dissent and change.*"[95] In fact, this view of authority applies to the Arab world like no other culture on earth—which is a catastrophe.

Take the subject of evolution, for instance. Authority, in this case religious authority, is fighting science to keep its version of the truth even if it contradicts the facts, common sense, and established scientific consensus. We know now that evolution is a settled scientific subject. For the most part, biology is the story of the science of evolution. Charles Darwin might well have been the most eminent genius who ever walked the earth. We all owe him a debt of gratitude. But, as usual, reality is not a welcome guest in all places. Some people wish things were otherwise. But to escape reality is to escape life and find refuge in delusional convictions. Some people dismiss evolution as "just a theory," which it is, although not in the way these mean. "Evolution is in fact a theory, a scientific theory. In everyday use, the word theory often means a guess or a rough idea. 'My theory is . . . ' 'I have a theory about that.' But among scientists, the word has an entirely different meaning. In science a theory is an overarching explanation used to describe some aspect of the natural world that is supported by overwhelming evidence."[96]

No civilization can afford to keep neglecting scientific theories based on evidence and remain relevant to modernity or progress. In this regard, once again, the Arab world is no exception. "The more we know of evolution, the more unavoidable is the conclusion that living things, including human beings, are produced by a natural, totally amoral process, with no indication of a benevolent controlling creator."[97]

The following 2009 Pew Research survey provides a useful indication of the diversity of religious opinions on the subject of evolution. Although it is confined to the US, it is telling in many ways. The numbers would surely differ if the same survey were undertaken in the Arab Middle East. It would certainly be lower than forty-five percent—perhaps in the range of Jehovah's Witness—in contrast to what it shows in the US Muslim community, which has been traditionally more liberal than its counterpart in the Arab world.

Religious Differences on the Question of Evolution

In advance of the 200th anniversary of Charles Darwin's birthday on Feb. 12, 2009, the Pew Research Center's Forum on Religion & Public Life recently released a research package exploring the evolution controversy in the U.S. The Pew Forum's U.S Religious Landscape Survey found that views on evolution differ widely across religious groups. (http://www.pewresearch.org/fact-tank/2015/11/17/5-facts-about-the-muslim-population-in-europe/)

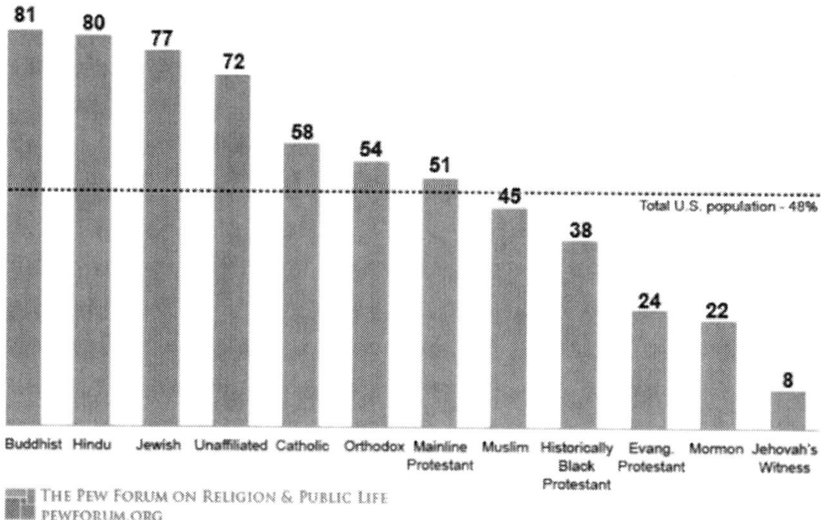

Totalitarianism and Freedom in the Arab World

Throughout its dramatic history, Russia has marched to quite a different drummer from the rest of the Western world. It never had an autonomous church; it missed the Reformation, the Enlightenment, the Age of Discovery, and modern market economics. Leaders with democratic experience are in short supply.

—Henry Kissinger in *Diplomacy*

The late Anwar Sadat even used to address the Egyptian people as "my children".

—The Middle East Quarterly, Fall 2002

If we replace the word "Russia" with "the Arab world," the above quote by Henry Kissinger, one of history's most prominent statesmen, would still represent the Arab state of affairs in the modern age. This very point was central to Mr. Ghassan Tueni's argument at the aforementioned debate in Beirut.

Arab political regimes were mostly authoritarian and despotic and spread their tyranny over the masses soon after colonialism ended and thereafter. A dark and vast security state system was implemented, covering every aspect of daily life, suffocating freedom, civil society, and liberal thinking, and, in the process, making the state a gigantic virtual prison.

Tueni put some of the blame on the educated elite, who were either afraid to challenge the state or were bought to remain silent. Either way, the Arab culture was in a sterile and destitute state for many decades—the lost decades since the end of the Second World War. To Tueni, the truth has four basic features, and Arab culture failed in many aspects and only copies others:

1. The usage of what humanity produces
2. Imitation: Copying Western civilization in most aspects
3. Trying to understand what one copies
4. Invention and modernization

Tueni concluded by calling for a cultural revolution in the Arab world and urged the new generation to stir things, move ahead of tradition, and to break through the chains of conformity, religious prohibitions, and suffocating political tyranny. Sure enough, the stirring and the storm started at the end of 2010 and continues today.

Arab Human Development Report 2002 and Freedom

> *"[Tyrannical] power is absolute, minute, regular, provident and mild. It would be like*

> *the authority of a parent if, like that authority, its object was to prepare men for manhood; but it seeks, on the contrary, to keep them in perpetual childhood: it is well content that the people should rejoice, provided they think of nothing but rejoicing. For their happiness such a government willingly labors, but it chooses to be the sole agent and the only arbiter of that happiness; it provides for their security, foresees and supplies their necessities, facilitates their pleasures, manages their principal concerns, directs their industry, regulates the descent of property, and subdivides their inheritances: what remains, but to spare them all the care of thinking and all the trouble of living?*
>
> *—Alexis de Tocqueville*

The deficit of freedom, along with the other two main deficits noted in the report—the deficit of knowledge and women's status—is of utmost importance in scanning the state of health of the Arab body politic. The report stated clearly that,

> This deficit, in the UNDP's interpretation, explains many of the fundamental things that are wrong with the Arab world: the survival of absolute autocracies; the holding of bogus elections; confusion between the executive and the judiciary (the report points out the close linguistic link between the two in Arabic); constraints on the media and on civil society; and a patriarchal, intolerant, sometimes suffocating social environment. . . . Democracy is occasionally offered, but as a concession, not as a right.[98]

The deficit of knowledge that the report summarized is scandalous. "The quality of education has deteriorated pitifully, and there is a severe mismatch between the labour market and the educational system. Adult illiteracy rates have declined but are still very high: 65m adults are illiterate, almost two-thirds of them women. Some 10m children still have no schooling at all."[99]

How can freedom exist, sink roots, and flourish when organized religion, political tyranny, and a backward educational system, plus illiteracy, coalesce to create a culture of catastrophe and callous disintegration? Today, we are witnessing this process in extreme forms at the hands of ISIS, religious fanatics, and barbaric state depots desperate to acquire and retain power at any cost, destroying their countries and millions of lives in the process.

Totalitarianism is rooted largely in a Machiavellian system of political thought. Freedom, morality, and ethics don't exist within that frame of political calculus. The tyrant who sucks the oxygen from civil society, from state institutions, and from the public and private spheres leaves nothing but a formula that proclaims, "Either me or chaos," "My life or death to all." As Leo Strauss says, "While freedom is no longer a preserve of the United States, the United States is now the bulwark of freedom. And contemporary tyranny has its roots in Machiavelli's thought, in the Machiavellian principle that the good end justifies every means."[100] Every despot in the Arab world has used this principle to justify the unjustifiable, to rule without consent, to commit unimaginable atrocities, and to rule for life and then transfer his illegitimate rule to his sons.

Culture and Freedom in the Arab World

We hold these truths to be self-evident: that all men are created equal; that they are endowed by their Creator with certain unalienable Rights; that among these are Life, Liberty and the pursuit of Happiness.

—Thomas Jefferson

My Lebanon, My Culture

Let us begin with Iraq, and then we will tackle Lebanon to give a cultural and traditional examination of an old question that came roaring back to the forefront after the US invasion of Iraq on March 20, 2003. The question is, "Was Iraq the way Iraq was (a dictatorship) because Saddam was the way Saddam was, or was Saddam the way Saddam was because Iraq was the way Iraq was—a collection of warring sects incapable of self-rule and only governable with an iron fist?"[101] In my opinion, this is the million-dollar question that must be answered about the Arab world in general. Many people blame Western imperialism and its utter disregard for the human rights of Arab citizens by aligning its policies with authoritarian regimes to secure its national interests, but this argument, although necessary, it is not sufficient to explain the indigenous forces and cultural factors that are at the heart of the historical cultural, political, moral, and economic decay visiting Arab lands in modern times.

Turning our attention to Lebanon, we can start to see some light through this tunnel. Take, for instance, the book written in 1870 by William M. Thompson, who recorded what he saw, experienced, heard, and studied during his stay in Lebanon.

He wrote the following telling analysis on the state of affairs at that time:

> Lebanon has about 400,000 inhabitants, gathered into more than six hundred towns, villages and hamlets . . . The various religions and sects live together, and practice their conflicting superstitions in close proximity, but the people do not coalesce into one homogeneous community, nor do they regard each other with fraternal feelings. The Sunnites excommunicate the Shiites—both hate the Druze, and all three detest the Nusairiyeh. The Maronites have no particular love for anybody and, in turn, are disliked by all. The Greeks cannot endure the Greek Catholics; all despise the Jews. . . . No other country in the world, I presume, has such a multiplicity of antagonistic races; and herein lies the greatest obstacle to any general and permanent amelioration and improvement of their condition, character, and prospects. They can never form one united people, never combine for any important religious or political purpose; and will therefore remain weak, incapable of self-government, and exposed to the invasions and oppressions of foreigners. Thus it has been, is now, and must long continue to be a people divided, meted out, and trodden down.[102]

Between 1870 and 2016, little, if any, significant changes occurred in the political culture in the land of the sun and olive trees called Lebanon! Mr. Thompson's description of Lebanon is still relevant for out times. The recurring trends are undeniable. The only changes we need to make are the names of the players and the different set of regional and international actors. But the melody, the beat, and the lyrics are virtually unchanged.

Summary

The cultural forces at play in the Arab world are the real movers and shakers of that region, which is going, yet again, through a historical period of turmoil and revolts that will decide the fate of more than 400 million inhabitants in twenty-two countries. History, religion, tradition, politics, geography, norms, gender status, social habits, thought, rationality, and superstition all make us wonder about the time and the music of history. The killing fields in Syria, Iraq, Yemen, Libya, and Lebanon remind us of how fragile and unpredictable the forces of culture and cultural decay really are.

Afterword

In July 2015, the Reputation Institute, which measures the reputation of 55 countries via an online panel of more than 27,000 people representing the G8 countries, published its new findings. The study measures sixteen attributes for each country, covering such things as: safety, beauty, friendliness of residents, progressive social and economic policies, effective governance, code of ethics, culture, and so on. On this scale, Canada received a score of 78.1, putting it in the lead right ahead of Norway, Sweden, Switzerland, and Australia. The United States was ranked number twenty-two out of fifty-five developed countries. Canada ranked the best for having an appealing environment, being a beautiful country, and having friendly and welcoming people. The top twenty most admired countries in the world were:

1. Canada
2. Norway
3. Sweden
4. Switzerland
5. Australia
6. Finland
7. New Zealand
8. Denmark
9. The Netherlands
10. Belgium
11. Ireland
12. Austria
13. UK
14. Italy
15. Germany
16. Japan

17. Spain
18. Portugal
19. France
20. Singapore

Needless to say, no country in the Arab world is in the developed category, so none of them appear anywhere on this list. But if the Reputation Institute were to consider the same formula and measurement for all the countries in the globe, it would be safe to assume, based on existing evidence of development and state of affairs, that the Arab world, which consists of twenty-two member states, would be at the bottom of the list regarding most of the criteria mentioned above.

Conclusions

Reformation: How to Fix Arab Cultural Crisis

The old strategies for growth and prosperity will no longer work. For too many people in too many places, the status quo today is unsustainable. In too many places, in too many ways, the region's foundations are sinking into the sand....those who cling to the status quo may be able to hold back the full impact of their countries' problems for a little while, but not forever.

—Hillary Rodman Clinton

"Traveler," says a Spanish proverb, "there are no roads. Roads are made by walking."

—Henry Kissinger from Diplomacy

The stone that we pushed to the peak is once again at the foot of the mountain. But we must push it back up, even with the knowledge that we can expect it to roll back down again.

—Gunter Grass, winner of the 1999 Nobel Prize for Literature

On October 28, 2007, one of the Arab world's best and most prominent writers, Samir Attallah, wrote an article in the Lebanese newspaper *Annahar* called "The Curse Is From Within," describing the plight of a tribe in Uganda called "Amba." This tribe is like no other in Africa. Historically, most African tribes believes that bad luck, curses, and misfortune comes from outside, from foreigners, but this tribe believes the opposite. They have developed a peculiar belief system that sees evil, curses, and deadly superstition as a product of people who are living within the tribe, within their neighbourhood and families.

This form of surreal superstition has created internal divisions, infighting, and catastrophic consequences to the body politic of the tribe, causing it to be weak and unable to survive. As a result, the Amba tribe was dispersed in the jungle into different sets of villages. Instead of creating a cohesive tribal union of villages to fight outside threats, they turned against each other instead, believing that curses, evil spirits, and bad omens come from within.

In many ways, and in many places, the Arab world is a modern-day version of the Amba tribe. A serious look at the state of the region provides nothing but despair, pessimism, and a dark outlook for generations to come. What can be done? What can emancipate the Arab world from this darkness, deadliness, and decay? If the Amba tribe in Uganda believed that the curse came from within, then the salvation must come from within as well! What might harm you could well be the antidote when the necessary adjustments are made. The question is, how?

In her *New York Times* review of author Ayaan Hirsi Ali's *Heretic*, Susan Dominus wrote this exceptionally relevant observation regarding the subject at hand. "Hirsi Ali is not merely looking to emphasize or reinterpret select scriptural passages: rather, she warns the reader that if Islam were a house, she would be going for a gut renovation, one that would 'make the outside look a lot like the original, but change the house radically from the inside."[103]

This total internal renovation includes structural domestic demolition on many fronts. Chief among them is the urgent task of dealing with and correcting the three "deficits" that the UN Arab Human Development Report 2002 warned about. These include lack freedom, knowledge, and freedom for women. Of course, the role of religion in society must also be addressed, and a minimum degree of separation of state and mosque must also be envisioned and practiced.

In his *New York Times* article, "Waiting for the Arab Spring of Ideas," Tariq Ramadan stated, "The Arab world, and Muslim-majority societies, need not only political uprisings, but also a thoroughgoing intellectual revolution from within that will open the door to economic change; to spiritual, religious, cultural and artistic liberation; and to the empowerment of women. The task is not an easy one."[104] This jihad from within, this renovation from inside, must be done with the "need to draw on Islamic traditions. Islam can be a fertile ground for political creativity—and not an obstacle to progress, as Orientalist thinkers in the West have so often claimed."[105] Westernized secular elites, although well intentioned, are not supported by the majority of middle class Arab societies. The idea of complete separation of religion and politics or the stand against any overlapping of religion and politics is actually a recipe for inaction and futility, because it runs against Islamic memories, tradition, and historical currents. Politics is the art of the possible. So, to change cultures, to change minds and hearts, pragmatism should be the first priority of any serious reformer. Change must be incremental. Change must come from within.

In my opinion, given Professor Ramadan's correct reading of the Arab state of affairs, the intellectual revolution must be initiated, supported, and directed by enlightened clergy and the religious establishment. Why? Because of the historical hold the religious narrative has had on the Arab culture and minds. Only through an enlightened and progressive group of elite religious leaders working in harmony and with a shared vision to promote this intellectual revolution from within Islamic heritage, historical realities, and cultural norms can the needed change occur. It cannot be imported or dictated or imitated. It must come from within the cultural landscape with the help of the clergy themselves. The question is, will the Arab world produce such an enlightened group of religious scholars who voluntarily relinquish power and privilege for the sake of building a new social contract, a better future, and a path to join the march of history?

A Marshall Plan for the Arab World

The most important political office is that of private citizen.

—Justice Louis D. Brandeis, US Supreme Court Justice

The accumulation of all powers, legislative, executive, and judiciary, in the same hands, whether of one, a few, or many, and whether hereditary, self-appointed, or elective, may justly be pronounced the very definition of tyranny.

—James Madison, Fourth US President

Academics who study the Arab world for a living were mostly surprised and bewildered that they failed to predict or at least warn of the coming upheaval in the advent of the Arab Spring. The persistence of totalitarianism and undemocratic rulers like Muammar al-Qaddafi in Libya, Ali Abdullah Saleh of Yemen, Hosni Mubarak of Egypt, Zine el-Abidine Ben Ali of Tunisia, the Assad family in Syria, and Saddam Hussein in Iraq all gave the myth of authoritarian stability a steady diet of food, water, and nourishment. But the veneer of normalcy was utterly misleading, because the fire was smouldering beneath the ashes of Arab tyrannical rulers.

Specialists in Arab politics now attribute their misunderstanding of the situation to three major overlooked forces: First, they underestimated the military's role in Arab political systems. Second, they misread the effects of economic change on political stability. Third, they underestimated the salience of a cross-border Arab identity.

> As paradigms fall and theories are shredded by events on the ground, it is useful to recall that the Arab revolts resulted not from policy decisions taken in Washington or any other foreign capital, but from indigenous economic, political, and social factors whose dynamics were extremely hard to forecast. In the wake of such unexpected upheavals, both academics and policymakers should approach the Arab world with humility about their ability to shape its future. That is best left to Arabs themselves.[106]

Fact: indigenous problems demand indigenous solutions. Democracy, development, and doors into modernity are not given as a gift or transported like a bouquet of flowers.

It is instructive to remember that the Arab world was ruled for about five hundred years by the Turkish Ottomans, who treated majorities and minorities as tools and suppressed them under their monopoly of power and politics in the region. Minorities like the Alawites, Christians, Jews, Druze, Shia, Kurds, and others were second-class citizens under a single rule. When the Ottoman Empire collapsed and disintegrated after World War One, France and Britain divided the Arab region into various entities and states like Syria, Iraq, Jordan, and Lebanon.

> So Sunnis, Shiites, Alawites, Christians, Druze, Turkmen, Kurds and Jews found themselves trapped together inside national boundaries that were drawn to suit the interests of the British and French. Those colonial powers kept everyone in check. But once they withdrew, and these countries became independent, the contests for power began, and minorities were exposed. Finally, in the 1960s and 1970s, we saw the emergence of a class of Arab dictators and monarchs who perfected Iron Fists (and multiple intelligence services) to decisively size power for their sect or tribe—and they ruled over all the other communities by force.[107]

Therefore, in hindsight, it is easy now to understand what happened since December of 2010 until today. The creation of these artificial states, fashioned by necessity or by unintended consequences, created artificial inhabitants of countries rather than genuine citizens. These different religious groups or competing sects were engaging in a tacit contract of mutual indifference, sharing political and geographical space but not necessarily religious, social, or moral space. "So what you are seeing today in the Arab awakening countries—Syria, Iraq, Tunisia, Libya, Egypt and Yemen—is what happens when there is no Iron Empire and the people rise up against the iron-fisted dictators. You are seeing ongoing contest for power—until and unless someone can forge a social contract for how communities can share power."[108]

Oh, that all-important social contract! How can the Arab world acquire it? Who is going to produce it? How can it be implemented after such bloodshed, bad history, and strife between these competing social and religious forces? The following Associated Press story should drive home this point.

> BAGHDAD: An attack by ISIS on a crowded marketplace in Iraq's eastern Diyala province

has killed 115 people, including women and children, in one of the deadliest single attacks in the country in the past decade.

The mostly-Shiite victims were gathered to mark the end of the Islamic holy month of Ramadan, which ended Friday for Iraqi Shiites and a day earlier for Iraqi Sunni Muslims.

Police said a small truck detonated in a crowded marketplace in the town of Khan Beni Saad Friday night in what quickly turned celebrations into a scene of horror, with body parts scattered across the market. At least 170 people were injured in the attack, police officials said, speaking anonymously because they are not authorized to brief the media.

Men quickly emptied boxes of tomatoes to use them for carrying the bodies of small children, witnesses said, while adult victims lay scattered around the attack scene waiting for medical assistance.

"Khan Bani Saad has become a disaster area because of this huge explosion," Diyala resident Sayif Ali said. "This is the first day of Eid, hundreds of people got killed, many injured, and we are still searching for more bodies."

ISIS claimed responsibility for the attack in a statement posted on Twitter accounts associated with the militant group.[109]

In the end, the religious schism between the Sunni and the Shia, between Islam and Christianity, between various sectarian groups in the Arab world, cannot be cured without a new Islamic enlightenment and reformation.

> It is high time, for starters, that Muslims were able to study the revelation of their religion as an event inside history, not supernaturally above it. . . . The traditionalists' refusal of history plays right into the hands of the literalist Islamofascists, allowing them to imprison Islam in their iron certainties and unchanging absolutes. If, however, the Koran were seen as a historical document, then it would be legitimate to reinterpret it to suit the new conditions of successive new ages. Laws made in the seventh century could finally give way to the needs of the 21st. The Islamic Reformation has to begin here, with an acceptance of the concept that all ideas, even sacred ones, must adapt to altered realities.[110]

Reformation or Recycled Revolts

> *Saddam did everything possible to evade the sanctions, diverting proceeds from the "oil-for-food" program (under which the Iraqi regime was allowed to sell just enough oil to buy food and medicine) into his own pocket and overseeing a vast operation smuggling oil across the borders into Iran for sale. He used a lot of that money to build dozens more gigantic, tasteless palaces that we would later occupy.*
>
> —*Robert M. Gates*

> *What we do know is that this extremist virus has taken root in a body that is already severely weakened and showing no signs of recovering soon.*
>
> *—David Ignatius*

One of the Arab world's most significant and consequential deficits is the absence of core elements of the social contract in most countries, if not all. Tribal, sectarian, familial, and individual interests trump all others. Because of this, the following scenario applies to the Arab state of affairs and summarizes to considerable degree the present dilemmas facing Arab lands:

> Assume that five men who have acquired a rudimentary ability to speak and to understand each other happen to come together at a time when all of them suffer from hunger. The hunger of each will be satisfied by the fifth part of a stag, so they "agree" to cooperate in a project to trap one. But also the hunger of any one of them will be satisfied by a hare, so, as a hare comes within reach, one of them grabs it. The defector obtains the means of satisfying his hunger but in doing so permits the stag to escape. His immediate interest prevails over consideration for his fellows.[111]

The notion of "me and my tribe, sect, or family above all else" is so ingrained into the social fabric of Arab societies that any mention of the broader social interest is taken as an abandonment of one's roots, heritage, or pride. Either rule or be ruled. Either me or the flood. In many ways, the Syrian and the Iraqi conflicts are embodiments of this axiom.

Reformation in the Arab world is as necessary to its survival as water is to humans lost in the desert. The list of items is long and urgent. However, here are some fundamental subjects as a starting point for cultural change:

1. Implement as soon as possible the recommendations and the roadmap to modernity contained in the United Nations Arab Human Development Reports from 2002 to 2005. The first report in 2002 was about the poor state of Arab development. Written by social scientists from the Arab world, it offered surgical analysis and a plan of action to restart the development process. The second report in 2003 was about the dismal state of Arab education and science. The third report in 2005 was about "the acute deficit of freedom and good governance," Plainly put, to escape this black hole, Arab political leaders, civil society organizations, the educated class, and the religious establishments must work together to implement the recommendations of these UN reports.

2. The reformation must start from an enlightened religious establishment. The clergy, or a special core group of respected religious persons, must lead a reformation in the reinterpretation of religious texts to accommodate and adapt to modernity. Arab culture has a history of *ijtihad,* which was functional for hundreds of years. As Reza Aslan writes on this subject: "The abiding nature of scriptures rests not so much in its truth claims as it does in its malleability, its ability to be molded and shaped into whatever form a worshiper requires."[112] It can be done again.

3. Women must be liberated for Arab societies to function properly. No other subject deserves more attention. I should include an important and urgent note in this regard: Read Emily Nasrallah's book *The Hostage,* written four decades ago. It deals with the state of women in the Arab world. This book is still banned in some Arab countries. With illiteracy as high as it is among women in Arab lands, and with the cultural disinterest in reading in

general, even if it were not banned, the odds for reform, change and progress are depressing and fleeting.

4. Education must be modernized. The knowledge-based economies of the world are a fact of life. To be competitive, productive, and able to create employment for millions of youth, which is of utmost importance, education systems throughout the Arab world must be dragged into the twenty-first century. For as Abraham Lincoln said in 1832, "Upon the subject of education, not presuming to dictate any plan or system respecting it, I can only say that I view it as the most important subject which we as a people can be engaged in."

5. Demography is destiny. The demographic trends in the Arab world are scary. This ticking bomb is of urgent concern. A plan of action must be implemented. Birth control programs must be given urgent priority.

6. Economic development and diversification must become a priority. Oil dependency is almost at the end of its time. A new vision of economic planning is a must. In fact, Arab culture is famous for its entrepreneurial energy and productive business community when conditions are ripe for action. But this must flow from political stability and social peace.

7. Kinship/tribalism loyalties must become a thing of the past. To join modernity, this traditional Arabic characteristic must end. It may take decades, but it must be tamed. Robert D. Putnam, a prominent American political scientist, wrote in *The New York Times* on June 12, 2012 that, "The most certain prediction that we can make about almost any modern society is that it will be more diverse a generation from now than it is today." Therefore, diversity, respect for minority rights, and accommodation of other groups and points of views are, and will continue to be, the defining features of our

times. The Arab world is lacking miserably on this front, and the current state of warfare within and without these states is telling and tragic.

8. The concept of citizenship must be introduced to all walks of life. Without citizens, there is no real state, no institutions, no social contract, and no social cohesion. In fact, a whole book could be dedicated to this vital subject. The disintegration of many Arab states is directly related to the utter lack of citizenship concept among the inhabitants of a certian geography. Syria, Iraq, Yemen, Libya, Somalia, and even Lebanon come to mind.
9. Separation of church and state is of utmost importance. No successful society can function without disentangling the web of politics and religion for the protection of both. Both are needed in different roles and responsibilities. Theocracies are destined to fail. Atheistic states are empty shells. Therefore, the formula of the Enlightenment is the best proven way envisioned by mankind thus far. That is, the realm of the religious and the secular each operating independently for the freedom of both within a shared social contract.
10. The freedom famine must end. A culture that does not respect and revere freedom in its fundamental features is bound to remain anemic and malnourished. Freedom is what makes the individual, the society, and the state tick. Freedom, properly practiced, rejects the destructive cultural practice of authority worship in the Arab world. Be it religious, political, or social, the cult of the individual is demeaning to human self-worth, self-esteem, and dignity.
11. A culture of critical thinking and reading must take root in Arab lands. Challenging dogma and established norms is never easy, but nothing moves forward without innovative and critical thinking outside traditional social

parameters, and that can only come about through an influx of new ideas. The Arab culture adors conformity and adherence to established system of thought, habits, and tradition. The need is so great for an innovative mind-set, for couragous intellectuals and for the new generation to utilize their education to change out-dated norms and ways of thinking. Translation of books, the World-Wide-Web and the information age may do that.

12. Freedom of religion must go hand in hand with freedom from religion. The truth is not limited to any established set of rules or ideas. Freedom is indivisible. Human liberty is the most valued human virtue. That culture of inclusivity must take root if there is to be any hope for things to change—and change we must.

In addition to the above, in her book *Heretic: Why Islam Needs a Reformation Now,* author Ayaan Hirsi Ali lists five things that must be transformed in order to achieve an Islamic Reformation, thus helping Arab Reformation in the process:

1. "Muhammad's semi-divine and infallible status along with the literalist reading of the Qur'an, particularly those parts that were revealed in Madina;

2. The investment in life after death instead of life before death;

3. Sharia, the body of legislation derived from the Qur'an, the hadith, and the rest of Islamic jurisprudence;

4. The practice of empowering individuals to enforce Islamic law by commanding right and forbidding wrong;

5. The imperative to wage jihad, or holy war."[113]

Change is inevitable in Arab lands, however dark and menacing the clouds appear and however discouraging the present upheaval seems. This same phenomenon occurred in Europe before the Reformation took shape. If history is any guide, there is light at the end of the tunnel. The Golden Age of Arab civilization can re-emerge again if the lessons of history are adopted, and if enlightened elites, both religious and secular, work in harmony to save themselves and this ancient and glorious culture.

"Imagine if," wrote Doug Saunders, "a century from now, we were to look back upon the Arab 2010s as something like the French 1790s or the American 1770s or the English 1640s — a terrible time that foretold the creation of a better time. To imagine this, you'd have to conclude the current Arab 'youth bulge' — the extraordinary proportion of the region's population (at least one-fifth) who are between 17 and 25...largely come to age, in a few years, as a new generation of adults seeking better economic and political futures." Endnote: Doug Saunders, "Banking on Arab youth to turn Arab countries around," *The Globe and Mail,* November 28, 2015.

Above all else, the Arab world needs to forge a détente between itself and modernity. It needs to move on cohabitation and then a bona fide marriage to have lasting peace.

The late Christopher Hitchens hit the nail on its head when he wrote the following unforgettable words:

> Above all, we are in need of a renewed Enlightenment, which will base itself on the proposition that the proper study of mankind is man, and woman. This Enlightenment will not need to depend, like its predecessors, on the heroic breakthroughs of a few gifted and exceptionally courageous people. It is within the compass of the average person. The study of literature and poetry, both for its own sake

> and for the eternal ethical questions with which it deals, can now easily depose the scrutiny of sacred texts that have been found to be corrupt and confected.[114]

The march of history is ever-lasting and ever-challenging to humankind. It knows no rules of engagement; it leaves no roadmap for the future. Each generation, each civilization must adapt, grow, or perish. The Arab civilization is no exception. As the following quote illustrates, history's meaning is in our hearts, minds, and actions: "The historian will not mourn because he can see no meaning in human existence except that which man puts into it; let it be our pride that we ourselves may put meaning into our lives, and sometimes a significance that transcends death. If a man is fortunate he will, before he dies, gather up as much as he can of his civilized heritage and transmit it to his children."[115]

This book has been an attempt to do just that. For, as Horace Mann said: "Until you have done something for humanity, you should be ashamed to die."

The "Great Certainty" is our undertaker and our fate. Hence life, reason, the pursuit of temporary happiness, writing, love, and laughing are our great and lasting revenge.

Endnotes

Introduction

1. Paul Kalanithi, "How Long Have I Got Left," *The New York Times,* January 24, 2014, http://www.nytimes.com/2014/01/25/opinion/sunday/how-long-have-i-got-left.html?_r=0. Dr. Kalanithi died of lung cancer at the age of 37. He was chief resident in neurology at Stanford University and a prolific and accomplished writer.
2. "Module I: Introduction." umanitoba.ca https://www.umanitoba.ca/faculties/arts/anthropology/courses/122/module1/culture.html (accessed November 25, 2015).
3. George F. Kennan, "The Sources of Soviet Conduct," *Foreign Affairs,* July 1947.
4. Janice G. Stein, "There is now humility and sober-mindedness about what outsiders can do," *Globe and Mail,* September 26, 2015, http://www.theglobeandmail.com/globe-debate/munk-debates/janice-stein-there-is-now-humility-and-sober-mindedness-about-what-outsiders-can-do/article26567935/.
5. Zbigniew Brzezinski, "The Wrong Way to Sell Democracy to the Arab World," *New York Times,* March 8, 2004, http://www.nytimes.com/2004/03/08/opinion/the-wrong-way-to-sell-democracy-to-the-arab-world.html.
6. Thomas Friedman, "Who Are We," *New York Times,* November 15, 2014, http://www.nytimes.com/2014/11/16/opinion/sunday/thomas-l-friedman-who-are-we.html.
7. Rebecca Newberger Goldstein, "Reasonable Doubt," *New York Times,* July 29, 2006, http://www.nytimes.com/2006/07/29/opinion/29goldstein.html.
8. "What is Orientalism?" Arab Stereotypes, http://www.arabstereotypes.org/why-stereotypes/what-orientalism (accessed November 24, 2015).
9. Costica Bradatan, "The Wisdom of the Exile," *New York Times,* August 16, 2014, http://opinionator.blogs.nytimes.com/2014/08/16/the-wisdom-of-the-exile/

10. Ibid.

Chapter 1

11. Office of the Deputy Chief of Staff for Intelligence US Army Training and Doctrine Command, "Arab Cultural Awareness." fas.org, https://fas.org/irp/agency/army/arabculture.pdf (accessed November 25, 2015).
12. Free Republic, "Understanding Arabic Culture," Freerepublic.com, http://www.freerepublic.com/focus/news/747968/posts (accessed November 25, 2015).
13. Costica Bradatan, "The Wisdom of the Exile," *New York Times,* August 16, 2014, http://opinionator.blogs.nytimes.com/2014/08/16/the-wisdom-of-the-exile/.
14. "Islamic Contributions to Civilization" *Baha'i Library Online,* http://bahai-library.com/cobb_islamic_contributions_civilization (accessed November 25, 2015).
15. Bernard Lewis, *What Went Wrong?* (New York: Perennial, 2002), 156.
16. Roger Cohen, "The Middle East Pendulum," *New York Times,* October 14, 2013, http://www.nytimes.com/2013/10/15/opinion/the-middle-east-pendulum.html.
17. Tara Bahrampour, "Review of Isobel Coleman's 'Paradise Beneath Her Feet,'" *Washington Post,* June 27, 2010, http://www.washingtonpost.com/wp-dyn/content/article/2010/06/25/AR2010062502162.html.
18. Thomas l. Friedman, "Tribes With Flags," *New York Times,* March 22, 2011, http://www.nytimes.com/2011/03/23/opinion/23friedman.html.
19. UNESCO-Beirut, Regional Officer for Education in the Arab States, "Literacy and Adult Education in the Arab World," UNESCO.org, http://www.unesco.org/education/uie/pdf/country/arab_world.pdf (accessed November 25, 2015).
20. "Average Arab reads 4 pages a year—UN survey" sputniknews.com, http://sputniknews.com/world/20081111/118255514.html (accessed November 25, 2015).
21. Ahmed Ksibi, "Promotion of reading in the Arab world," ifla.org, http://www.ifla.org/files/assets/libraries-for-children-and-ya/publications/Ahmed-reading-arab.pdf (accessed November 25, 2015).
22. Bernard Lewis, *What Went Wrong?* (New York: Perennial, 2002), 159.

Chapter 2

23. Gilbert Achcar, *The People Want: A Radical Exploration of the Arab Uprising* (Oakland: University of California Press, 2013), 22.

24. Bernard Lewis, *What Went Wrong?* (New York: Harper Perennial, 2002), 156.

25. Hillel Ofek, "Why the Arabic World Turned Away from Science," *New Atlantis,* Winter 2011, http://www.thenewatlantis.com/publications/why-the-arabic-world-turned-away-from-science.

26. Ibid.

27. Ibid.

28. Ibid.

29. Ibid.

30. Thomas L. Friedman, "Arabs Life Their Voices," *New York Times,* April 7, 2005, http://www.nytimes.com/2005/04/07/opinion/arabs-lift-their-voices.html.

31. Hillel Ofek, "Why the Arabic World Turned Away from Science," *The New Atlantis,* Winter 2011, http://www.thenewatlantis.com/publications/why-the-arabic-world-turned-away-from-science.

32. Niall Ferguson, *Civilization: The West and the Rest* (London: Penguin Press, 2011), 305–306.

33. "Germany—Language, Culture, Customs and Business Etiquette," Kwintessential.co.uk, http://www.kwintessential.co.uk/resources/global-etiquette/germany-country-profile.html (accessed November 25, 2015).

34. "Values & Proverbs," Depauw.edu, http://academic.depauw.edu/mkfinney_web/teaching/Com227/culturalPortfolios/germany/Values.htm (accessed November 25, 2015).

Chapter 3

35. Fareed Zakaria, "Why they still hate us, 13 years later," *The Washington Post,* September 4, 2014, https://www.washingtonpost.com/opinions/fareed-zakaria-why-they-still-hate-us-13-years-later/2014/09/04/64f3f4fa-3466-11e4-9e92-0899b306bbea_story.html.

36. "Illiteracy rife among rural Egyptian girls and women," *Daily Star,* March 13, 2006, http://www.dailystar.com.lb/News/Middle-East/2006/Mar-13/68476-illiteracy-rife-among-rural-egyptian-girls-and-women.ashx.

37. Ibid.

38. Thomas L. Friedman, "It's Not Just About Us," *The New York Times,* October 9, 2012, http://www.nytimes.com/2012/10/10/opinion/friedman-what-romney-didnt-say.html.

Chapter 4

39. Friedrich Huebler, "Adult and youth literacy in 2010," huebler.blogspot.ca, http://huebler.blogspot.ca/2012_05_01_archive.html (accessed November 25, 2015).

40. "The Big Read," Campaignforeducation.org, http://www.campaignforeducation.org/bigread/en/ (accessed November 25, 2015).

41. Reza Aslan, "Bill Maher Isn't the Only One Who Misunderstand Religion," *New York Times,* October 8, 2014, http://www.nytimes.com/2014/10/09/opinion/bill-maher-isnt-the-only-one-who-misunderstands-religion.html.

42. Tom Fletcher, "So . . . Yalla, bye, dear Lebanon," Foreign & Commonwealth Office, http://blogs.fco.gov.uk/tomfletcher/2015/07/31/19389/comment-page-2/ (accessed November 25, 2015).

43. Thomas L. Friedman, "ISIS, Boko Haram and Batman," *New York Times,* October 4, 2014, http://www.nytimes.com/2014/10/05/opinion/sunday/thomas-l-friedman-isis-boko-haram-and-batman.html.

44. Thomas L. Friedman, "ISIS and SISI," *New York Times,* June 24, 2014, http://www.nytimes.com/2014/06/25/opinion/thomas-friedman-isis-and-sisi.html.

45. David Brooks, "No War Is an Island," *New York Times,* July 28, 2014, http://www.nytimes.com/2014/07/29/opinion/david-brooks-when-middle-east-conflicts-become-one.html?mtrref=www.google.ca&gwh=2A38F3AD5E7C3F2F6371A3CCD992D0DF&gwt=pay&assetType=opinion.

46. Thomas L. Friedman, "Close to the Edge," *New York Times,* August 20, 2013, http://www.nytimes.com/2013/08/21/opinion/friedman-close-to-the-edge.html.

47. Will and Ariel Durant, *The Lessons of History* (New York: Simon and Schuster, 1968), 50.

48. Dr. Ahmad FDr. Ahmad F..Yousif, "Revisiting Religious Freedom, Minorities, and Islam: A Challenge to Modern Theory of Pluralism," in 1998-2011 (1st and 2nd eds.).

49. Ibid.

50. Scott M. Thomas, "A Globalized God: Religion's Growing Influence in International Politics," *Foreign Affairs,* November/December 2010, 97–98.

Chapter 5

51. Karrie Kehoe, "Factbox: Women's rights in the Arab world," Reuters.com, http://www.reuters.com/article/2013/11/12/us-arab-women-factbox-idUSBRE9AB00I20131112 (accessed November 25, 2015).

52. Scott MacLeod, "What's Holding Back Arab Women?" *Time*, December 7, 2006, http://content.time.com/time/world/article/0,8599,1567155,00.html.

53. Ibid.

54. Ibid.

55. Ibid.

56. Ibid.

57. Thomas von der Osten-Sacken and Thomas Uwer, "Is Female Genital Mutilation an Islamic Problem?," *Middle East Quarterly,* Winter 2007, http://www.meforum.org/1629/is-female-genital-mutilation-an-islamic-problem.

58. UNICEF, "Female Genital Mutilation/Cutting," Childinfo.org, http://www.childinfo.org/files/FGCM_Lo_res.pdf (accessed November 25, 2015).

59. Ibid.

60. Thomas von der Osten-Sacken and Thomas Uwer, "Is Female Genital Mutilation an Islamic Problem?," *Middle East Quarterly,* Winter 2007, http://www.meforum.org/1629/is-female-genital-mutilation-an-islamic-problem.

61. "A Brief History of the Veil in Islam," Facinghistory.org, https://www.facinghistory.org/for-educators/educator-resources/readings/brief-history-veil-islam (accessed November 25, 2015).

62. Nicholas D. Kristof, "Religion and Women," *New York Times,* January 10, 2010, http://www.nytimes.com/2010/01/10/opinion/10kristof.html?mtrref=www.google.ca&gwh=10B9637AE5E315DA7146329D6AC9FBAE&gwt=pay&assetType=opinion.

63. Ibid.

64. Reza Aslan, "Bill Maher Isn't the Only One Who Misunderstand Religion," *New York Times,* October 8, 2014, http://www.nytimes.com/2014/10/09/opinion/bill-maher-isnt-the-only-one-who-misunderstands-religion.html.

Chapter 6

65. Rukmini Callimachi, "ISIS Enshrines a Theology of Rape," *New York Times,* August 13, 2015, Kttp://www.nytimes.com/2015/08/14/world/middleeast/isis-enshrines-a-theology-of-rape.html?_r=0.

66. Amira El Ahl and Daniel Steinvorth, "Love, Lust and Passion: Sex and Taboos in the Islamic World," *Spiegel International,* October 20, 2006, http://www.spiegel.de/international/spiegel/love-lust-and-passion-sex-and-taboos-in-the-islamic-world-a-443678.html.

67. Martin Chukov, Elieen Byrne and Abdul-Rahman, "After the Arab spring, the sexual revolution," *Guardian,* April 27, 2012, http://www.theguardian.com/world/2012/apr/27/after-arab-spring-sexual-revolution.

68. Will and Ariel Durant, *The Lessons of History* (New York: Simon and Schuster, 1968), 40–41.

69. Frank Bruni, "Catholicism Undervalues Women," *New York Times,* May 6, 2015, http://www.nytimes.com/2015/05/06/opinion/frank-bruni-catholicism-undervalues-women.html.

70. Ibid.

71. John Gray, *Mars and Venus in the Bedroom* (New York: HarperCollins, 1995), 1.

72. Robert Sibley, "Magna Carta: The 'Essence' of the West," *Ottawa Citizen,* June 13, 2015, http://ottawacitizen.com/news/national/magna-carta-the-essence-of-the-west-or-irrelevant-scrap-of-paper.

Chapter 7

73. Thomas L. Friedman, "Pass the Books. Hold the Oil," *New York Times,* March 10, 2012, http://www.nytimes.com/2012/03/11/opinion/sunday/friedman-pass-the-books-hold-the-oil.html.

74. Fareed Zakaria, "Why Saudi Arabia can't get a nuclear weapon," *Washington Post,* June 11, 2015, https://www.washingtonpost.com/opinions/saudi-arabias-nuclear-bluff/2015/06/11/9ce1f4f8-1074-11e5-9726-49d6fa26a8c6_story.html.

75. Ibid.

76. Eman El-Shenawi, "Poking at the Beast: How much is the Arab world worth?" *Al Arabiya News,* May 5, 2011, http://english.alarabiya.net/articles/2011/05/05/147980.html.

77. Tina Rosenberg, "Avoiding the Curse of the Oil-Rich Nations," *New York Times,* February 13, 2013, http://opinionator.blogs.nytimes.com/2013/02/13/avoiding-the-curse-of-the-oil-rich-nations/.

78. Ian Williams, "Despite U.S., Israeli Pressure, Arab Human Development Report Faults Occupations," in *Washington Report On Middle East Affairs,* July 2005, http://www.wrmea.org/2005-july/united-nations-report.html.

Chapter 8

79. "The challenged kingdom," *The Economist,* May 23, 2015, http://www.economist.com/news/briefing/21651829-new-leaders-saudi-arabia-want-increase-its-clout-they-face-hard-task-challenged.

80. "Difference Between Education and Learning," Differencebetween.net, http://www.differencebetween.net/miscellaneous/difference-between-education-and-learning/ (Accessed November 25, 2015).

81. James Coffman, "Does the Arabic Language Encourages Radical Islam," *Middle East Quarterly,* December 1995, http://www.meforum.org/276/does-the-arabic-language-encourage-radical-islam.

82. Ibid.

83. Gerry Spence, *How to Argue and Win Every Time* (New York: St. Martin's Press, 1995), 100.

84. Kahlil Gibran, *The Prophet* (New York: Alfred A. Knopf, 2008), 60.

Chapter 9

85. "The Tragedy of the Arabs," *The Economist,* July 5, 2014, http://www.economist.com/news/

leaders/21606284-civilisation-used-lead-world-ruinsand-only-locals-can-rebuild-it.

86. Ronald Johnson, "Arabs," *Encyclopedia of World Cultures,* 1996, http://www.encyclopedia.com/topic/Arabs.aspx.

87. "Arabic Culture," *The Free Dictionary,* http://encyclopedia2.thefreedictionary.com/Arabic+Culture (accessed November 25, 2015).

Chapter 10

88. Edward W. Said, *Culture and Imperialism* (New York: Vintage Books, 1994), 301.

89. Pew Research Center, "The Great Divide: How Westerners and Muslims View Each Other," *Pew Research Center,* June 6, 2006, http://www.pewglobal.org/2006/06/22/the-great-divide-how-westerners-and-muslims-view-each-other/ (accessed November 25, 2015).

90. Ibid.

91. Ibid.

Chapter 11

92. Pew Research Center, "The Great Divide: How Westerners and Muslims View Each Other," Pewglobal.org, http://www.pewglobal.org/2006/06/22/the-great-divide-how-westerners-and-muslims-view-each-other/ (accessed November 25, 2015).

93. Margaret Wente, "Why the niqb matters, now and in the future," *Globe and Mail,* September 29, 2015, http://www.theglobeandmail.com/globe-debate/why-the-niqab-matters-now-and-in-future/article26573582/.

94. Anne Applebaum, "Putin's Power Plays," *Washington Post,* September 27, 2015, https://www.washingtonpost.com/opinions/what-putin-will-do-to-stay-in-power/2015/09/27/12a964b0-63b7-11e5-8e9e-dce8a2a2a679_story.html.

95. Michael P. Lynch, "Wittgenstein and Philosophy," *New York Times,* June 6, 2013, http://opinionator.blogs.nytimes.com/2013/03/05/of-flies-and-philosophers-wittgenstein-and-philosophy/.

96. Karen Barss, "Human Evolution," Factmonster.com, http://www.factmonster.com/ipka/A0932663.html (accessed November 25, 2015).

97. David P. Barash, "God, Darwin and My College Biology Class," *New York Times,* September 27, 2014, http://www.nytimes.com/2014/09/28/opinion/sunday/god-darwin-and-my-college-biology-class.html.

98. "How the Arabs Compare: Arab Human Development Report 2002," *The Middle East Quarterly,* Fall 2002, http://www.meforum.org/513/how-the-arabs-compare .

99. Ibid

100. Leo Strauss, *Thoughts on Machiavelli* (Chicago: University of Chicago Press, 1958), 13–14.

101. Thomas l. Friedman, "Iraq's Known Unknown, Still Unknown," *New York Times,* February 24, 2010, http://www.nytimes.com/2010/02/24/opinion/24friedman.html.

102. William M. Thompson, *The Land and the People* (New York: Harper and Brothers, 1870).

Conclusions

103. Susan Dominus, "Ayaan Hirsi Ali's 'Heretic,'" *New York Times,* April 1, 2015, http://www.nytimes.com/2015/04/05/books/review/ayaan-hirsi-alis-heretic.html.

104. Tariq Ramadan, "Waiting for an Arab Spring of Ideas," *New York Times,* September 30, 2012, http://www.nytimes.com/2012/10/01/opinion/waiting-for-an-arab-spring-of-ideas.html.

105. Ibid.

106. F. Gregory Game III, "Why Middle East Studies Missed the Arab Spring," *Foreign Affairs,* Jul/Aug 2011, 81–90. Game is a professor of political science at the University of Vermont.

107. Thomas L. Friedman, "Iron Empires, Iron Fists, Iron Domes," *New York Times,* December 5, 2012, http://www.nytimes.com/2012/12/05/opinion/iron-empires-iron-fists-iron-domes.html.

108. Ibid.

109. Associated Press, "Anger in Iraq after suicide attack on marketplace kills 115," *Daily Star,* July 18, 2015, http://www.dailystar.com.lb/News/Middle-East/2015/

Jul-18/307243-anger-in-iraq-after-suicide-attack-on-marketplace-kills-115.ashx.

110. Salman Rushdie, "The Right Time for An Islamic Reformation," *Washington Post,* August 7, 2005, http://www.washingtonpost.com/wp-dyn/content/article/2005/08/05/AR2005080501483.html.

111. Kenneth W. Waltz, *Man the State and War* (New York: Columbia University Press, 1959), 176–178.

112. Reza Aslan, "Bill Maher Isn't the Only One Who Misunderstands Religion," *New York Times,* October 8, 2014, http://www.nytimes.com/2014/10/09/opinion/bill-maher-isnt-the-only-one-who-misunderstands-religion.html.

113. Ayaan Hirsi Ali, *Heretic: Why Islam Needs A Reformation Now* (Toronto: Alfred A. Knopf Canada, 2015), 24.

114. Christopher Hitchens, *God is not Great: How Religion Poisons Everything* (Toronto: Emblem, 2007), 283.

115. Will and Ariel Durant, *The Lessons of History* (New York: Simon and Schuster, 1968), 102.

CPSIA information can be obtained at www.ICGtesting.com
Printed in the USA
LVOW08s2350220616

493757LV00005B/49/P

9 781460 282786